Far from the Madding Crowd

Thomas Hardy

1994
Hong Kong
Oxford University Press
Oxford Singapore Tokyo

KU-435-799

Oxford University Press

Oxford   New York   Toronto
Kuala Lumpur   Singapore   Hong Kong   Tokyo
Delhi   Bombay   Calcutta   Madras   Karachi
Nairobi   Dar es Salaam   Cape Town
Melbourne   Auckland   Madrid

and associated companies in
Berlin   Ibadan

Oxford is a trade mark of Oxford University Press

First published 1994

© Oxford University Press 1994

Retold by L.A. Hill

Illustrated by Wu Siu Kau

Syllabus designer: David Foulds

Text processing and analysis by Luxfield Consultants Ltd.

ISBN 0 19 586317 8

Printed in Hong Kong
Published by Oxford University Press (Hong Kong) Ltd
18/F Warwick House, Taikoo Place, 979 King's Road,
Quarry Bay, Hong Kong

CONTENTS

BATHSHEBA EVERDENE

Beautiful but vain

Farmer Gabriel Oak was twenty-eight and not yet married.

One morning, as he was walking along the road near his sheep farm on Norcombe Hill, a cart drove past him. It was piled high with furniture, and on top of it all sat an attractive-looking girl.

Suddenly the cart stopped for a moment. The pretty girl took a small mirror from a bag, looked at herself in it, smiled happily, and then blushed.

Oak watched. He could see that she was not looking at herself for any good reason, but only to remind herself that she was beautiful. Doubtless she was dreaming of future victories over men, he thought.

The cart started along the road again, and Gabriel, who was walking in the same direction, followed it. At the toll-gate, where people had to pay to go on along the next section of the road, the gatekeeper and the young woman began to argue. They were having a disagreement over a difference of twopence.

Oak did not think that it was worth arguing about such a small amount of money. He said to the man at the toll-gate,

'Here's twopence. Let the young woman pass.' Then he looked up at her, but she looked away.

Gabriel was not handsome, but he was not ugly either. The girl turned to look back at him carelessly, and then told the driver to drive on. She did not thank him. By paying for her, Gabriel had spoilt her fight with the other man, and women do not like such favours.

'That's a beautiful girl,' said the toll-gatekeeper.

'But she has faults,' said Gabriel.

'True. Arguing over money, like that.'

'No. She is vain,' answered Farmer Oak.

The cowshed

It was nearly midnight on Norcombe Hill, not far from where Gabriel had seen the beautiful girl a few days before. All was quiet. Suddenly the sound of a flute broke the silence. The music came from a shepherd's hut. The hut, and the flute, belonged to Gabriel Oak.

Oak had begun as a shepherd by helping his father look after flocks of sheep that belonged to some rich landowners. During the past year he had saved enough money to rent a small sheep farm, and he was now a master, not an employee. He had bought two hundred sheep to start with, but he had not yet paid for them. He did not employ anyone to help him.

The flute-playing stopped, and Farmer Oak came out of his hut, carrying a lamp. He walked about the hillside, making sure that his sheep were safe and well. Then he stood looking at the sky, first to work out the time from the stars, and then just to enjoy its beauty.

As he watched, he began to realize that something he had thought was a star, low down among some trees, was actually a light coming from a lamp.

He walked towards it. He remembered that there was a shed there, and as he approached, he could see that the light was coming from cracks in the wooden walls.

Quietly, he looked in. There were two women and two cows in the shed. One of the women was past middle age, but the other was young and graceful, although Gabriel could not see her face.

'Well, we'll go home now,' the older woman said. 'I hope Daisy will get better soon. I've never been more frightened in my life.'

'I wish I hadn't lost my hat,' the younger woman said. 'The wind blew it over the hedge, I think.'

'We need some more food for the cows,' said the elder woman.

'Yes, aunt. I'll ride over to get it as soon as it's light.'

Oak had been trying all this time to see the younger woman's face. Now by good luck she turned, and he recognized her at once as the girl in the cart.

The two women took their lamp and went down the hill. Gabriel returned to his flock.

The clever rider

The next morning, Gabriel went back to the cowshed. As he stood there thoughtfully, he saw a horse approaching. The rider was the young woman of the night before. Gabriel remembered the hat she had lost, and thought that perhaps she had come to look for it. He quickly searched the ditch, and soon found it. Then he took it back to his hut, and looked out through a hole in the direction of the approaching horse.

He was just going to go out and give the girl her hat when something strange stopped him. The girl had to ride under the low branches of some trees, and after looking around quickly to be sure that no one was watching, she dropped backwards flat on the horse and went under the branches like that. Then she rode away. Gabriel was astonished — and amused.

An hour later, the girl came back with a sack of hay for the cow. She went into the shed with a milking bucket, and soon Gabriel could hear her milking the cow. He took her lost hat, and waited outside.

When she came out, he was able to look at her carefully for the first time. She was as attractive as he had thought.

5 She was surprised to see Gabriel standing there. When she saw him examining her face, she brushed it with her hand, as if Gabriel had touched it with his, but she did not blush. Gabriel did.

'I found a hat,' said Oak.

10 'It's mine,' she said. 'It flew away last night.'

'One o'clock this morning.'

'Well — it was.' She was surprised. 'How did you know?'

'I was here.'

15 'Oh, you are Farmer Oak, aren't you?'

'That's right.'

'I wanted my hat this morning,' the girl went on. 'I had to ride to get food for a sick cow.'

'Yes, you did.'

20 'How do you know?'

'I saw you.'

'Where?' she asked, looking worried.

'Here — going through the wood, and down the hill.'

The girl remembered lying back on her horse, and now

25 she blushed. Gabriel turned his head politely, and when he looked again, she had gone back into the cowshed. He returned to his work, half happy and half sad.

Gabriel nearly dies

Five days passed. Each day the young woman came to

30 look after the cows, but she never looked at Gabriel. She had been deeply offended — not because he had seen her behaviour on the horse, but because he had told her that he had seen it. The way she avoided him made him feel something for her that he had not been conscious of

35 before. He liked her well enough to miss her.

Then one evening the weather changed, and it became
very cold. As the time for milking the cows approached,
Oak watched the cowshed as usual, but after a while he
felt too uncomfortable to stay outside. He went into his
hut. To keep the icy wind out, he closed all the air holes.   5
Soon he fell asleep. How long he remained like that he
never knew, but when at last he began to wake, slowly,
he realized he was lying on the ground outside the hut.
He could hear one of his dogs howling, and he could feel
that someone was loosening the collar of his shirt.

When he opened his eyes, he
was surprised to see that his head
was on the lap of the beautiful
girl, and her fingers were
unbuttoning his collar.

'Whatever is the
matter?' he said.

She seemed slightly amused.
'Nothing now,' she answered, 'as you're not dead.
But it's surprising that you weren't killed in that hut of   20
yours. There's no air in there. It was silly of you to close
all the air holes when your stove was alight.'

'Yes — I suppose it was,' said Oak. He was enjoying
the feeling of being so close to her.

'How can I thank you?' he said at last, gratefully.   25
'Oh, never mind that,' she answered with a warm smile.
'How did you find me?'

'I heard your dog howling.'

'I believe you saved my life, Miss — I don't know your name.'

'I'd prefer not to tell you. There's no reason why I should, either, as you will probably never see me much again.'

'Well, I thank you. Come, give me your hand!'

She hesitated, but then did as he asked. He held it only for a moment, afraid to seem too bold.

'I'm sorry,' he said.

'What for?'

'Letting your hand go so quickly.'

'You may have it again if you like. There it is.' She gave him her hand again.

Oak held it longer this time. 'How soft it is,' he said. 'It isn't rough or red because of the winter.'

'There — that's long enough,' she said, though without pulling it away. 'But I suppose you're thinking you'd like to kiss it? You may if you want to.'

'I wasn't thinking of any such thing,' said Gabriel simply, 'but I will —'

'You won't!' she objected, and pulled her hand back quickly.

Gabriel felt that he had been stupidly rude again.

'Now find out my name,' she said teasingly, and left.

A lamb for Bathsheba

Young Oak's love for the pretty girl soon grew. Every morning he found himself waiting eagerly for her to appear. But the girl did not show any interest in him. He found out that her name was Bathsheba Everdene, and that she was staying with her aunt, Mrs Hurst. He also found out that the cow she came to milk each day would become dry in about seven days, and then Bathsheba would not come any more to milk it. He feared the arrival of the eighth day.

At last the eighth day came. The cow stopped giving milk for that year, and Miss Everdene did not come up the hill any more.

Gabriel's suffering increased as each day passed without him seeing Bathsheba. In the end he decided that he could only stop it by marrying her.

Now he had to think of a good reason for going to her aunt's house. His chance came when one of his sheep died, shortly after giving birth to a lamb. Oak put the lamb in a basket and crossed the fields to Mrs Hurst's house. He knocked at the door, feeling nervous.

Bathsheba's aunt came to the door. 'Will you tell Miss Everdene that somebody would like to speak to her?' said Mr Oak, trying to be very formal.

Bathsheba was not in, the aunt said.

'I've brought a lamb for Miss Everdene,' said Gabriel. 'I thought she might like to look after it. But I really came to ask her to marry me. Do you know if she has any other young men?'

'Yes, certainly,' said Mrs Hurst. 'There must be a dozen. She's beautiful — and clever, you see.'

'That's unfortunate,' said Farmer Oak, looking down-heartedly at the floor. 'I'm just an ordinary sort of man. My only real chance was to be the first. Well, it's no use my waiting, because that was all I came for, so I'll go home.'

Gabriel's offer of marriage

When Gabriel had gone just a short way, he heard a shout behind him. He looked round, and saw the girl running towards him. He stopped, and waited.

'Farmer Oak — I —,' Bathsheba said, stopping to get her breath back. 'I didn't know you'd come to ask me to marry you, or I would have talked to you. I've come to say that my aunt was wrong when she said I'd already got a young man. I haven't. I've never had one.'

'I'm glad to hear that,' said Farmer Oak happily. He tried to take her hand, but she quickly put it behind her back. 'I have a nice comfortable little farm,' said Gabriel, feeling rather less confident.

5   'Yes, you have.'

'I borrowed the money to buy it, but it will soon be paid off. I've been quite successful in my work. I'm quite sure that when we're married, I can work twice as hard as I do now.'

10   Gabriel put out his arm to hold her hand again, but Bathsheba stepped back away from him.

'I never said I would marry you!' she objected.

'Well, that isn't reasonable!' said Oak unhappily. 'To run after somebody like that — and then say you don't want
15   him!'

'I only wanted you to know I don't have a young man yet, instead of having a dozen, as my aunt said. If I'd wanted you, I wouldn't have run after you. That would have been too immodest. But there was nothing wrong in
20   hurrying to correct what my aunt had said.'

'Well, I'm not quite so sure about that.'

'I didn't have time to think whether I wanted to marry you or not.'

Gabriel was happier now. 'Well, think for a minute or
25   two. Will you marry me? I love you very much.'

'I'll try to think,' she said, hesitating. 'Give me time.' She stood there silently for some minutes, and then said, 'No, I don't want to marry you. A wedding would be nice and I wouldn't mind becoming a bride. But I don't want a
30   husband.'

'That's a stupid thing to say,' Oak answered. He sighed, and after a pause, went on, 'Why won't you have me?'

'Because I don't love you. And I'm too independent. I want someone who can tame me, and you would never
35   be able to do that.' There was another long pause while Oak looked away hopelessly, and then the girl added, 'I have no money at all, and I'm better educated than you.

You're a farmer who's just beginning. You ought to marry a rich woman.'

'You know, I've often said exactly that to myself!' Farmer Oak answered without thinking.

'Then why did you come and bother me?' Bathsheba said, almost angrily.

'What I think would be wise is one thing, but I just can't do it.'

'Do you think I could marry you, after you say such things?'

Gabriel was angry now. 'Don't misunderstand me like that!' he objected. 'Saying that you aren't good enough for me is nonsense. I've heard that your uncle at Weatherbury is a large farmer — much larger than I'll ever be. Won't you think about my offer some more?'

'No — no — I cannot. I don't love you!' she said with a laugh.

No man likes it when people laugh at his feelings, so Gabriel said firmly. 'Well, I won't bother you again then.'

Misfortunes

One day soon afterwards, Gabriel heard news of the departure of Bathsheba Everdene. This only strengthened his love for her. He heard that she had gone to Weatherbury, which was nearly twenty miles off, but he could not discover if she had gone there as a visitor, or permanently.

Soon after this he suffered a great misfortune. The younger of his two dogs, too eager at his work, started Gabriel Oak's sheep running. Thinking he was doing the right thing, the dog drove them faster and faster towards the far end of Norcombe Hill, where there was a chalk pit. In their panic, many sheep fell over the edge into the pit. It was a steep drop. Two hundred of them died.

Later that day, Gabriel shot the dog, but he had to sell everything he owned to pay his debts.

2

WEATHERBURY

Casterbridge fair

Two months later, a great fair was held in the town of
Casterbridge. It was held once every year, and it had
become famous as an occasion for hiring workers. That
5 year there were two or three hundred workers there, all
looking for jobs. Many of them were carrying the tools of
their trade: the cart drivers carried whips, the shepherds
crooks, and so on.

Gabriel was there, too. He was hoping to get an
10 appointment as a bailiff — a farm manager, but all the
farmers and landowners seemed to want shepherds.

He decided to buy a shepherd's crook. He had no
money, so he took his flute out of his pocket, sat beside
the road, and began to play. Soon people stopped and
15 gave him money for his music, and when he had enough
he went to a shop and bought a crook. But when he got
back to the fair, the farmers seemed to have changed their
minds. Now they wanted bailiffs, not shepherds, so he
had no luck.

20 He heard that the next day there would be another fair,
this time at Shottsford. Shottsford was ten miles beyond
Weatherbury.

Gabriel remembered that Bathsheba had gone to
Weatherbury, but he thought she had probably left there
25 long before this. However, he decided to walk to
Weatherbury that evening, spend the night there, and go
on to Shottsford Fair the following day.

As he approached Weatherbury, he noticed that
something was on fire. When he got a little closer, he saw
30 that it was a big rick of straw burning in a farmyard.

Gabriel finds work

Gabriel jumped over a hedge and began to run towards
the farmyard. He was not the only one there. One man
was hurrying about and shouting to others for help. Soon
a large number of people were running this way and that   5
in confusion, not really knowing what to do.

Gabriel knew. He took command, and got someone to
bring him a thick cloth to hang between the burning rick
of straw and the other ricks. Then he made the man stand
beside the cloth with a bucket of water to keep it wet.   10

After that Oak got a ladder, climbed onto the rick that
was next to the burning one, and began using his crook
to beat off the small burning pieces that had blown onto
it from its neighbour.

Watching all this were two women, one of them on a   15
horse, and the other on foot.

'He's a shepherd,' said the woman on foot. 'I can see
his crook. A fine young shepherd, too, madam.'

'Whose shepherd is he?' said the one on the horse.

'I don't know, madam. Nor do any of the others here.'   20

'Is the barn safe from the fire?'

'I don't know. I'll ask. She turned to the nearest man and asked the same question.

'Yes, it is now,' he answered. 'The shepherd up there
5 did the most to save it.'

'Maryann,' said the woman on the horse, 'when the shepherd comes down, go and say that the farmer wants to thank him for the great service he has done.'

Maryann went off and did this.

10 'Where is your master, the farmer?' said Oak as he came down the ladder.

'It isn't a master. It's a mistress.'

'A woman farmer?'

'Yes, and a rich one, too,' said one of the men. 'She
15 arrived here recently, and took over her uncle's farm when he died suddenly.'

Oak walked over to the woman on the horse. Her face was covered with a veil against the smoke. He took off his hat respectfully, and said in a hesitating voice, 'Would
20 you perhaps want a shepherd, madam?'

She lifted the veil. Gabriel was very surprised. The woman on the horse was Bathsheba Everdene.

Bathsheba did not know whether to be amused by the strangeness of this meeting, or worried because it was so
25 awkward. She felt a little pity for Gabriel, too, and a good deal of pride in herself.

'Yes,' she said quietly, trying to look important, 'I am thinking of hiring a shepherd. But …'

The other workers at once urged her to take Gabriel.
30 After a moment's thought Bathsheba said, 'Very well, you can work for me. Go and speak to Mr Pennyways, the bailiff.' Then she rode away into the darkness.

The thin girl

After he had made arrangements with the bailiff, Gabriel
35 went to find lodgings. Mr Pennyways had told him to try

Warren's Malthouse, which was the largest inn at Weatherbury. On his way there, he came to a place where there were some trees growing beside a high wall. He noticed someone standing there in the darkness, but as he was walking silently on soft grass, that person did not notice him. Gabriel accidentally kicked a stone, and the person moved. It was a thin girl, wearing thin, summer clothes.

Gabriel said, 'Good evening,' and the girl answered his greeting in an unexpectedly attractive voice.

'Is this the right way to Warren's Malthouse?' Gabriel asked, partly because he really wanted to know, but mostly because he wanted to hear that voice again.

'Yes,' the girl answered. She hesitated, and then said, 'Do you know when the Buck's Head Inn closes?'

'I don't know anything about that. Are you going there tonight?'

'Yes —' the girl paused again. 'You aren't a local man then?'

'No. I'm the new shepherd at Weatherbury Farm.'

'Oh,' the girl answered. 'Only a shepherd? You look more like a farmer.'

'Just a shepherd,' Oak repeated sadly, thinking of the past.

'Please don't tell anyone that you saw me here,' the girl then said. 'I'm rather poor, and I don't want people here to know about me.' Then she was silent and shivered.

'You ought to be wearing a cloak on such a cold night,' said Oak. 'I would advise you to go indoors.'

'Oh, no — could you please leave me now? Thank you very much.'

'I will go.' He hesitated and then added, 'Perhaps you would accept a little money from me. It's only a shilling, but that is all I can spare.'

'Yes, I will take it,' the girl answered gratefully.

As Gabriel put his hand out in the darkness to touch hers. He noticed the girl's pulse was beating terribly fast.

'What's the matter?' he said.

'Nothing.'

'But there is!'

'No, no! There's nothing wrong. Good night.'

Gabriel left, feeling that he had been close to a very deep sadness.

At the inn

Oak found Warren's Malthouse and went in. The first person he noticed was the owner, a very old man with white hair and a white beard. Many of the other men there were workers from Bathsheba's farm, and they welcomed Gabriel warmly. They were all drinking from one big, dirty old mug, which was now passed to Gabriel so that he could drink, too.

The men drank and talked, and when there was a pause, Gabriel asked, 'What sort of a place is this to work in? And what kind of a mistress is she to work for?'

'We know very little about her,' said one man. 'She only arrived here a few days ago. Her uncle died, and she's going to have the farm, people say.'

'Yes,' said another man. 'Her uncle was a good, fair man. He was not married, and she is his only living relative.'

'And did any of you know Miss Everdene's father or mother?' Oak asked.

'They lived in a town, not here,' the owner of the inn said. 'He was a tailor, and quite rich, people say. But they've been dead for years.'

'I remember her as a child,' said another. 'She wasn't at all pretty. I would never have thought that she would become such a beautiful woman.'

'I hope that her temper is as good as her face,' said someone else.

'Yes, but we'll have more to do with the bailiff than with her I expect, and he isn't a nice man.'

They talked and drank for a while, and then someone   5
noticed Gabriel Oak's flute sticking out of his pocket. They asked him to play for them, and Gabriel agreed.

After the first piece of music, a young man said, 'He plays very well. I wish I could do that, too.'

'But it's a pity that a man has to screw his mouth up   10
in such an ugly way to play the flute,' said another.

Someone else whispered to Gabriel, 'I hope you don't mind that young man's bad manners.'

'Not at all,' answered Oak.

'Because you're really a handsome person,' the man   15
continued.

'Thank you very much,' Gabriel answered. But he decided that he would never let Bathsheba see him playing the flute.

The bailiff dismissed   20

Soon afterwards the men began to leave. One of them offered Gabriel lodgings, but before they could go, one of those who had left earlier ran back in.

'Miss Everdene has caught Pennyways stealing sacks of corn and has dismissed him,' he said. 'The question now   25
is, who's going to be the next bailiff?'

Then another man ran in.

'Have you heard the news?' he asked.

'About Pennyways?'

'No, more than that.'   30

'What's that?'

'Fanny Robin, Miss Everdene's youngest servant, has disappeared. She'd been in very low spirits for some time, and people are afraid that she may be dead. Miss Everdene wants to speak to us all before we go to bed.'   35

They all hurried to the farmhouse, and saw Bathsheba's head and shoulders at her bedroom window.

'Tomorrow morning, two or three of you must go round the villages and ask whether Fanny Robin has been seen,' she said to them. 'Do it quietly, so as not to frighten people.'

'Does Fanny have a man friend?' asked someone.

'I don't think so,' answered Bathsheba. 'The thing that worries me is that Maryann saw her go out without her coat on.'

Maryann was looking out of another window, and now she said, 'Fanny did have a man friend once, but he lives in Casterbridge. I think he's a soldier.'

'I can go there tomorrow and ask the army people,' one man said.

'Yes, do that,' Bathsheba answered.

Gabriel Oak left with the others. That night, in his lodging, he remained awake for an hour or more, thinking tenderly of Bathsheba.

Mistress and men

The next morning, Bathsheba and her servant-companion, Liddy, were working in the farmhouse, sorting through some papers and rubbish that Bathsheba's uncle had left. A visitor called. His name was Boldwood. He was a gentleman farmer who had a farm nearby. He had come to ask if anyone had heard anything about Fanny. Mr Boldwood had helped Fanny when she was a child, and he was worried about her.

Bathsheba was dirty and untidy from her work. She said she could not see him. Later she found out from Liddy that Mr Boldwood was unmarried, about forty, handsome and rich. However, Liddy added, 'He's a hopeless man for a woman! Many have tried to marry him, but none have succeeded.'

Liddy asked Bathsheba if anyone had ever wanted to marry her. Bathsheba thought of Gabriel Oak. She said a man had wanted to marry her once, but he wasn't good enough for her, and she had refused him.

'Did you love him, Miss,' Liddy asked?   5

'Oh, no, but I rather liked him.'

'Do you still like him?'

'Of course not — but who's that?'

Footsteps could be heard outside, and when they looked out of the window, the two women could see a   10 long line of the farm workers. They had come for the weekly meeting when they received their wages.

'Go down and keep them in the kitchen till I have dressed,' said Bathsheba, 'and then I'll come down and see them in the hall.'   15

Half an hour later Bathsheba, now properly dressed, and followed by Liddy, arrived in the hall, where all her men were sitting on benches. She sat at a table, took out the book in which everyone's working hours were written, opened a cloth money-bag, and poured some coins out   20 of it.

'Now, first of all men,' said Bathsheba, 'I have something to say. The first thing is I have dismissed Mr Pennyways for stealing, and am going to do his work myself. I shall be my own bailiff.'   25

The men gasped in surprise.

'The second thing is, have you heard anything of Fanny?'

Several men told her about their attempts to find the girl. One said that the man who had gone to Casterbridge   30 to look for her boyfriend had not come back yet.

Bathsheba then began to pay the men their wages. She gave each man ten shillings more than usual, to celebrate her taking over the farm. They were highly surprised about this. She also asked each man his name, what he   35 did on the farm, and whether he wanted to remain now that she had taken over. All of them said that they did.

FARMER BOLDWOOD

No news of Fanny

Heavy footsteps were heard outside the hall door, and the man who had gone to Casterbridge to look for Fanny Robin's boyfriend arrived.

5 'I would have come sooner if the weather had not made it so difficult. It has been snowing quite hard,' he said.

'What can you tell us about Fanny?' asked Bathsheba.

'Well, madam, she's run away with the soldiers.'

'No — not a steady girl like Fanny!'

10 'Yes, her boyfriend's regiment has been moved to another town, and she has gone with it.'

'Did you find out the boyfriend's name?'

'No, madam, nobody knows.'

'Well, one of you can run over in a minute and tell
15 Farmer Boldwood.'

Then Bathsheba stood up and said a few words to her men in a quiet and serious way that was made even more striking by the black dress she was wearing. She was in mourning clothes, because of the death of her uncle.

20 'You now have a mistress instead of a master,' she said. 'I shall do my best, as a farmer, and if you serve me well, I shall serve you in the same way. Don't think that because I am a woman, I don't understand the difference between what is good and what is bad.'

25 'No, madam,' they all answered.

'And so good day to you all.'

'Good day, madam.'

Outside the barracks

On the evening of the same day, but many miles north of
30 Weatherbury, a small human shape could be seen moving

slowly through the snow along a public path, beside a river. On the far side of the river was a high wall.

Through the darkness and the falling snow, one could just see windows in this wall, and the small shape was counting these: 'One. Two. Three. Four. Five.' 5

The figure then bent down, picked up some snow and threw it, but it missed the window. Again another throw, and another, till the wall was a mass of lumps of snow. At last one piece hit the window, but nothing happened.

One more successful throw, and this time the window 10 opened, and a voice called out, 'Who's there?'

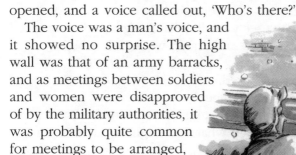

The voice was a man's voice, and it showed no surprise. The high wall was that of an army barracks, and as meetings between soldiers and women were disapproved of by the military authorities, it was probably quite common for meetings to be arranged, like this one, across the river at night.

'Is that Sergeant Troy?' the shape on the path said in a trembling voice.

'Yes,' the man's voice from the window answered suspiciously. 'Who are you?' 25

'Oh, Frank — don't you know me? I'm your wife, Fanny Robin.'

Making arrangements

The man at the window was clearly taken by surprise.

'Fanny! Is that really you?' he called out in complete 30 astonishment.

'Yes,' the girl said, her voice shaking with deep feeling. Neither she nor the man seemed to be speaking in the way one expects between a husband and a wife.

'How did you get here?' the man asked. 35

'I asked which was your window. Forgive me!'

'I did not expect you tonight. Actually, I did not think that you would come at all. It's surprising that you found me here. I'm on duty tomorrow.'

5   'You told me to come.'

'Well, I said that you might.'

'Yes, I mean that I might. You're glad to see me, Frank?'

'Oh, yes, of course.'

'Can you come to me?'

10   'My dear Fanny, no! The gates have been closed for the night. For us it is like being in prison till tomorrow.'

'Then I shan't see you till then!' The girl's voice trembled in disappointment. 'And Frank, when will it be?'

'What?'

15   'What you promised.'

'I don't quite remember.'

'Oh, you do! Don't speak like that. It makes me terribly sad. It makes me say what you ought to say first.'

'All right, say it.'

20   'Oh, must I? It's this: when are we going to be married?'

'Oh, I understand. Well, you have to get the right clothes first.'

'But, I have no money, Frank. And we have to get an announcement from your church and mine. Will you
25   arrange that tomorrow with your church?'

'Not tomorrow. In a few days.'

'And have you the permission of your officers?'

'No — not yet.'

'But you told me you almost had before you left
30   Casterbridge!'

'Well, I forgot to ask. Your arrival like this is so sudden and unexpected.'

'Yes — yes — it was wrong of me to worry you. I'll go away now. Will you come and see me tomorrow at
35   Mrs Twill's house in North Street? I don't want to come to the barracks. Bad women come here like this, and I don't want people to think that I am one.'

'Yes, I'll come to see you, my dear. Good night.'

'Good night, Frank — good night!'

The small shape moved away, the window closed, and then men's laughter could be heard coming from inside.

At the corn market

The first public sign of Bathsheba's decision to run her farm herself came when she went to the corn market at Casterbridge.

All the other farmers there were big, heavy men, and the arrival of a young woman in pretty clothes made everyone stop talking and look at her. It needed more determination than she had expected to appear there.

As she discussed business with tall men, the boldness of her face showed she had the courage to do whatever she wished, but her eyes were always soft. When arguing about prices, she always kept to her own firmly, as one must do in business, and pushed the other person's down, as women can always do. But she was never obstinate or mean.

Some of the farmers at the market did not know who she was, and asked others.

'Farmer Everdene's niece,' was the answer. 'She has taken Weatherbury Farm on, and dismissed the bailiff. She says she'll do everything herself.'

Others shook their heads. 'It's a pity she's so hard,' they said to one another. 'But we ought to be proud of her. She brightens up the old place.'

In fact, all the men at the market were filled with admiration for her, both as a businesswoman and because of her beauty. She was sometimes tempted just to walk among them proudly like a queen, and to neglect prices completely. But there was one exception to this general admiration. Bathsheba did not know who he was, but he was between thirty-five and fifty years old, tall, quiet and, above all, dignified.

Afterwards, as she drove home in her small carriage with Liddy, she learned that the man was her neighbour, Farmer Boldwood. Bathsheba had not seen him until her visit to the corn market. She thought he was a very
5 handsome man, but she wondered why he did not seem to be interested in the people and things around him.

The valentine

That Sunday afternoon Liddy and Bathsheba were at home, in the farmhouse, talking.
10 'Did you notice Mr Boldwood in church this morning, miss?' Liddy asked. 'He sat exactly opposite your place, but he didn't turn to look at you once.'
'Why should he?' said Bathsheba. 'I didn't ask him to.'
'Oh, no, but everyone else was looking at you.'
15 There was a long silence, and then Bathsheba said, 'Oh, I'd nearly forgotten the valentine card that I bought yesterday.'
'A valentine? For whom, miss? For Farmer Boldwood?'
'Well, no. It was for Mrs Coggan's little boy. I've
20 promised him something, and this will be a nice surprise.'
Liddy said it would be more fun to send the valentine to Farmer Boldwood. In the end Bathsheba agreed, but as she addressed the envelope, she yawned to show that she did not care very much who received the card.
25 Then they had to choose a seal for the envelope. There were several different ones in Bathsheba's uncle's desk. She chose one that had some small writing on it.
When she had finished the sealing, she looked at the still hot red wax and wrote the words 'MARRY ME' in it.
30 The valentine was sent. Bathsheba thought no more of it. She had quite often seen love, but she had no direct experience of it at all.
On the evening of St Valentine's Day, Boldwood sat down for his supper. The valentine card was in front of
35 him on the shelf above the fire. It was too far away for

him to be able to read the
words on the seal, but he
knew that they said:
  'MARRY ME'
  Bathsheba had
sent the valentine
light-heartedly, but
in this house it had
become something
deeply serious. Since
receiving the card that morning, Boldwood had
felt his quiet life gradually moving towards deep feelings.

Of course he did not know that the valentine had been
sent with the least possible feeling. He did not even
imagine that this was possible.   15

When he went to bed, he put the valentine in the corner
of his mirror, and it was in his mind even when he had
his back to it. It was the first time that anything like this
had ever happened to him. He did not know who had
sent it, but again and again he tried to imagine the   20
woman's face as she wrote those two words on the seal.

That night he dreamt of her, and in the morning he
went out and walked to the gate of one of his fields. He
was standing there thinking, when the postman came and
gave him a letter. Boldwood opened it eagerly, expecting   25
that it would be a note from the person who had sent the
valentine. He was disappointed to discover that the
postman had made an error. The letter was for Gabriel.

Boldwood decided to take the letter to Warren's
Malthouse, where he hoped to find Oak. He wanted to   30
give him the letter and to explain that he had opened it
in error.

Talking about the new mistress

The owner of the inn and some of Bathsheba's men were
having breakfast at Warren's Malthouse.   35

'How's your mistress doing without the bailiff?' the owner asked.

'She's sure to regret it,' answered one of the men with a bitter smile.

5 'We'll all be ruined,' said another man. 'She knows very little about farming.'

'Yes, and she refuses to listen to advice,' said someone else. 'She's proud and vain.'

Loud, firm footsteps were now heard outside. The door 10 was suddenly kicked open, and Mr Oak came in. He was carrying four lambs over his shoulders, and was followed by his dog, George. He wrapped the newly-born lambs in hay, and put them near the fire.

'We haven't got a hut for the new lambs yet,' he said 15 to the owner of the inn, 'and it's a long way to take them back to the farm. If I couldn't bring them here when the weather's like this, I don't know what I'd do.'

'Sit down, shepherd,' the owner answered. 'The men have been talking about the strange things the new mistress is doing.'

'What have they been saying about her?' Oak said angrily.

'They say she's proud and vain.' Oak said, 'I don't allow such talk. Who said these things?'

He asked each man in turn, and each of them answered that he had not said anything.

'Well, somebody has,' Gabriel went on. 'Here's my fist.' He put it on the table. 'Now, the first man that I hear saying bad things about our mistress will smell and taste this!'

Nobody spoke, until one said, 'She ought to have appointed you bailiff.'

'I must admit that I expected it,' Oak answered honestly. 'But she also has a right to be her own bailiff if she wants.' He looked at the table sadly, and sighed, but this had nothing to do with the appointment he had hoped for, and did not get.

The warmth of the fire now brought the lambs to life and they began to cry out, so Oak gave them some milk.

Farmer Boldwood arrives

Just then Boldwood came in.

'Ah, Oak,' he said, 'I thought you might be here. The postman brought this letter. I opened it, but I think it is really for you. Please excuse me.'

'That's all right, Mr Boldwood,' said Gabriel at once. He took the letter and read it. It was from Fanny Robin, and was to thank him, and to tell him that she was going to marry Sergeant Troy soon. She was sending back the shilling Gabriel had given her, because her husband would object to her accepting money from others, except as a loan.

'He is a very respectable man of high honour,' the letter went on. 'Indeed he is a nobleman by blood.'

The letter then asked Oak to keep what she had written a secret, as she and the sergeant hoped to surprise Weatherbury, where he had lived as a child, by coming there soon as man and wife.

'If you haven't read this letter, Mr Boldwood, you'd better do so. I know you are interested in Fanny Robin,' Oak said.

Boldwood read the letter and looked sad.

'Poor Fanny! What she wants hasn't happened yet — and it may never happen.'

MARRIAGE PROBLEMS

The truth comes out

Gabriel wanted to know what sort of man Sergeant Troy was. He learned that Troy was not someone that a person would trust, though he was clever. His mother was a
5 French woman who came to look after the children of an important family who lived near Weatherbury. She and Lord Severn had had an affair. Later she married a poor medical man, and soon after that a baby — Sergeant Troy — was born. When he grew up, he began work as a
10 lawyer's clerk, but then he joined the army for some reason. People rather doubted that he would marry Fanny.

Just then Cain Ball, Oak's assistant shepherd, ran in to say that two more lambs had been born. Oak picked up some of the lambs in the inn, and made Cain carry the
15 others, and they hurried away. Boldwood followed them out and showed Gabriel the valentine card.

'Do you know whose writing this is?' Boldwood asked, pretending that he was not very interested.

Oak looked and blushed.

20 'That's Miss Everdene's writing,' he said.

He had blushed because he had been made to think of Bathsheba, but now a new thought worried him. The card could not, of course, have been signed, or Boldwood wouldn't have needed to ask. Perhaps he had given away
25 a secret.

Boldwood saw that Oak was worried, but he thought it was for another reason.

'It was perfectly fair of me to ask you,' he said. 'Everyone knows, when they send such cards, that the
30 people who get them will try to find out who sent them. That's the fun of it.'

Actually, knowing who had sent the valentine was not giving Boldwood much 'fun'. He went home, feeling ashamed and sorry that he had shown his feelings to a stranger by asking him that question.

Late for her wedding

At All Saints Church, in the town where Sergeant Troy's barracks were, the morning service had just finished. Most of the people who had been at it were women or girls, and they were getting ready to leave when they saw a sergeant in a red uniform come in. He looked very embarrassed, but was trying to hide this by walking fast.

He went up to the priest and whispered something to him, and then the priest whispered to his clerk.

'There's going to be a wedding,' some of the women said quietly. 'Let's wait.' They sat down.

The church clock struck half past eleven, and one of the women whispered, 'Where's the bride?'

The sergeant stood without moving, and minutes passed. The clock struck a quarter to twelve, and the women began to laugh quietly.

Time passed, and when the clock struck twelve, the priest left, and so did the clerk. The sergeant had not yet turned round. Every woman wanted to see his face, and he seemed to know this. At last he did turn and walked bravely back to the church door.

Outside was a square, and the young man was crossing it when he met a thin, little woman going in towards the church.

The man fixed his eyes on her in silent anger and asked, 'What happened?'

'Oh, Frank, I made a fearful mistake. I went to the wrong church. I was there at exactly half past eleven, as you said. I waited till a quarter to twelve, and then found I was at All Souls instead of All Saints. But I wasn't very frightened, because I thought it could just be tomorrow.'

'You are a fool for treating me like this.'

'Will it be tomorrow?'

'Tomorrow!' He laughed rudely. 'I won't let a thing like that happen to me again for quite some time, I promise you!'

'But the mistake wasn't such a terrible thing!' she argued in a trembling voice. 'Now, dear Frank, when will it be?'

'Ah, when? God knows!' he answered shortly, and walked quickly away.

Bathsheba has regrets

Bathsheba did not know that Boldwood was deeply serious about everything. If she had, she would have blamed herself severely for the way in which she had stirred up feelings in him that had never been stirred before. If she had known what power she now had over him, she would have trembled at the responsibility she had taken on.

One day, when Farmer Boldwood had gone out into his fields to look at his animals, he noticed Bathsheba in her fields, not far away. He decided to go and speak to her, but when he drew closer, he pretended that he was just passing. Bathsheba realized what he had really intended. She felt sorry that she had made it seem she was the sort of person who played with men's feelings.

She decided never again in any way to interrupt this man's life. But such decisions are usually made too late, when it is impossible to carry them out.

At last one day Boldwood called at Bathsheba's house, but she was not at home. She had gone to see the sheep being washed. He went to look for her.

The pool for washing sheep was a circular arrangement of brick walls at the side of a small river. Several men were doing the washing. Two of them were up to their waists in the water, pulling the sheep in. Gabriel was pushing the animals right under the water with a long pole

as they swam along. They swam against the current, so
that the dirt was washed out of their wool, and they came
out clean at the other end.

Boldwood came along, and said, 'Good morning.'
Bathsheba thought he had just come to watch the sheep
being washed. She walked away, further along the river
bank, but Boldwood followed. Soon they were completely
round the bend of the river, behind a hedge. They could
not be seen by the others there, but they could still hear
the shouting and splashing of the sheep washing.

'Miss Everdene,' the farmer began hesitantly. 'I feel —
almost — too much — to think.' Then in an unusually
soft voice he said. 'I have come to make you an offer of
marriage.'

Bathsheba was surprised, and found it difficult to
answer. In the end she said, 'Though I respect you very
much, Mr Boldwood, I do not feel I can accept such an
offer.'

'My life is nothing without you,' Boldwood continued
in a quiet voice. 'I want you to let me say that I love you
— again and again. I hope you care enough for me to
listen.'

Bathsheba wondered why he hoped this, but then
remembered the valentine.

'I'm sorry to have to tell you that I am afraid I cannot
marry you. You are too dignified for me to suit you, sir,'
she said. 'I should not have sent you that valentine. It was
very thoughtless of me. If you will pardon me, I promise
never to —'

'No, no, it was not thoughtless. I am rich enough to
look after you in every way. You will never need to work
or worry about anything. God only knows how much this
means to me!'

'Don't say that, Mr Boldwood! I cannot bear you to feel
so much, and me to feel so little. Give me time to think.'

'Say then that you do not absolutely refuse. May I speak
to you again?'

'Yes. But do not hope to marry me.'
'Can I come again tomorrow?'
'No, you must give me longer.'

A quarrel

5   Bathsheba thought deeply about Boldwood's offer. She
knew that most women would have accepted such a man
eagerly. She knew, too, that she was the one who had
started the whole thing, but she felt that she could not
marry him.

10   The next day the sheep shearing began. Bathsheba
went to the end of the garden, where Gabriel Oak was
sharpening the shears on the grindstone, while his
assistant, Cain Ball, turned the handle.

'Cain,' Bathsheba said, 'go down to the lower field and
15   fetch the brown horse for me. I want to speak to Gabriel.'

Cain went, and Bathsheba took the handle of the
grindstone. Gabriel had looked up in surprise, but now
looked down again. Bathsheba turned the handle,
and Gabriel sharpened the shears.

After a few minutes, Bathsheba
found that the work of turning the
grindstone stopped her thinking,
so she said, 'You can turn now,
Gabriel, and I'll sharpen. I
came to ask you if the men
said anything about my
going behind the hedge with
Mr Boldwood yesterday.'

'Yes, they did … You aren't
holding the shears right, miss.'

He went over, put his hands over hers
and turned the shears a little sideways.

He held her hands for rather a long time,
until she said, 'That's enough! Take your
hands off mine. I don't want you to hold them.'

Gabriel went back to the handle, and Bathsheba said again, 'Did the men think that it was strange?'

'More than that. They said they expected you and Farmer Boldwood to marry before the end of the year.'

'I came to see you because I want you to tell the men that that is foolish and not true. They must have heard what Mr Boldwood said to me.'

'Well, if he really spoke of marriage, I'm not going to tell a lie and say that he didn't. I've already tried to please you too much for my own good.'

Bathsheba was surprised. She did not know whether to pity him for his disappointed love, or be angry with him for not loving her any more.

'I just want you to say that it is not true that I am going to marry him,' she said quietly, feeling less confident.

'I could say that to them, Miss Everdene, and I could also tell you what I think of what you have done.'

'I don't want your opinion.'

But as they went on with their work, she changed her mind. 'Well, what is your opinion?' she asked.

'That to behave in such a way is not worthy of any nice, thoughtful woman.'

Bathsheba said nothing, but her face became an angry red. Then Gabriel made a serious mistake. 'Perhaps you don't like the rudeness of my scolding,' he said, 'but I thought it might do some good.'

'No, on the contrary, the opposite is true. I have such a low opinion of you that when you think something is bad, it means that sensible people must think it is good.'

It was clear that Bathsheba had lost her temper, and for that reason Gabriel remained quite calm. He said nothing, and then she went on, 'May I ask why you think I am not a worthy person? Is it because I refused to marry you?'

'Oh, no. I stopped thinking about that a long time ago.'

'Or wishing it, I suppose.'

It was clear that she expected him to say, 'No' to this at once, but he just repeated her words, 'Or wishing it.'

Bathsheba would have allowed Gabriel to criticize her as much as he liked if he also said that he still loved her. This is what she had expected. But to be criticized coolly and without love was too much for her.

5   Gabriel had not finished. 'My opinion is that you are greatly to blame for playing tricks on Mr Boldwood.'

'I won't allow anyone to say such critical things about my private behaviour!' she said. 'Please leave the farm at the end of the week!'

10   'All right, I will,' said Gabriel calmly. 'I would prefer to go now.'

'Go at once then!' she answered with flashing eyes. 'I don't want to see your face here any more.'

'All right, Miss Everdene.' And he took his shears and
15   left in a quiet and dignified way.

'Do not leave me'

On Sunday afternoon, twenty-four hours after Gabriel Oak had left, a group of Bathsheba's workers ran up to the farmhouse.

20   One of them shouted out, 'Some sheep have broken the fence and got into a field of young clover — about sixty of them. Their stomachs are filling with gases and they'll all die if no one does anything to help them.'

'Oh, what fools! Get them out of there quickly,' exclaimed
25   Bathsheba, and she ran to the clover field with the men.

Most of the sheep in the clover field were lying down. They could not move, their stomachs were so large because of the clover gases. They had to be lifted out of the field. Those that could still walk were driven out into
30   the next field, where several more fell down after a few minutes and lay there helpless.

'There's only one way of saving them,' said one of the men.

'What? Tell me quickly!' exclaimed Bathsheba, shocked
35   at seeing so many animals in such pain.

'You have to stick a special instrument into their sides.'

'Can you do it? Can I?'

'No, madam. It must be done in exactly the right place. If you go even a fraction of an inch to the right or left, you kill the sheep. Only one man in this part of the country knows how to do it, and that's Shepherd Oak.'

'How dare you say that name in front of me!' exclaimed Bathsheba angrily. Then her face brightened and she said, 'Farmer Boldwood will know!'

'Oh, no, madam,' said one of the other men. 'Two of his sheep had the same trouble a few days ago, and he sent for Gabriel, who saved them.'

'Well, go and find someone to help!' said Bathsheba.

The men all left, while she stayed behind.

'I'll never send for him — never!' she said firmly to herself, as she stood among the dying sheep.

Suddenly one of them jumped high in the air, fell back heavily to the ground, and lay dead.

She could still see one of her farm workers in the distance, and she called to him.

'Where is Oak staying?' she asked.

'Across the valley at Nest Cottage.'

'Take the brown horse, ride across, and tell him that he must come immediately. Tell him I said so.'

The man left, and after some time she saw him coming back.

'What a fool!' she said. 'Why didn't he let Gabriel ride the horse?'

The man arrived. 'Shepherd Oak says that beggars can't be choosers,' he told Bathsheba. 'In other words, he says he won't come unless you ask him politely, like a woman who is begging a favour.'

'What rudeness! Oh, he has no respect for me at all!' Bathsheba said angrily.

Another sheep jumped up into the air and fell dead. Bathsheba began to cry bitter tears. She saw where her pride and obstinate behaviour had led her.

All the men had come back now.

'There's no need to cry, miss,' said one. 'Why don't you just ask him nicely? He's a kind man.'

Bathsheba went back to the farmhouse, and wrote: 'Do not leave me, Gabriel' on a piece of paper. She gave it to one of the men and told him to take it to the shepherd.

An anxious quarter of an hour later, Gabriel arrived on the brown horse. He was not angry. His face showed no feelings of any kind. Bathsheba, on the contrary, looked at him with grateful eyes and said, 'Oh, Gabriel, how could you treat me so unkindly?'

Gabriel did not answer. They both hurried to the field. There he took the instrument for letting the gases out of the sheep's stomachs from his pocket and began work. He carefully chose the right place on each sheep's body, and then stuck the point of the instrument into its skin. Forty-nine operations were performed successfully; one failed, and the sheep died, because Gabriel was having to hurry. Four sheep had already died before he could get to them.

When it was all finished, Bathsheba came and looked at Oak's face.

'Gabriel, will you stay with me?' she said with a winning smile.

'I will,' Gabriel answered.

She smiled at him warmly again.

5

SERGEANT TROY
APPEARS AGAIN

The sheep shearing

All was now ready for the sheep shearing to begin.
Bathsheba watched carefully to see that none of the sheep
were cut with the shears, and Gabriel sometimes did some
of the shearing himself, and sometimes watched and   5
helped the others. He was very happy to be so close to
his mistress, although he felt no need to talk to her. She
did all the talking, which really meant nothing, and he
was silent, which meant a lot.

This pleasant arrangement was suddenly and painfully   10
interrupted by the arrival of Farmer Boldwood. He came
towards Bathsheba, and she turned to greet him. Then
they spoke together, quietly.

Gabriel could not hear what they were saying. He did
not want to go nearer to listen, but he was too concerned   15
to take no notice of it. Were they only talking about the
shearing? Gabriel thought that they were not. Usually
when someone is talking about something, he or she looks
at it. But Bathsheba had her eyes fixed on the ground the
whole time. Oak could see that she was blushing, and   20
looking uncomfortable. He went on working, feeling sad.

Bathsheba left Boldwood, and walked about alone for
nearly a quarter of an hour. Then she went away, and
came back in her riding clothes with one of the men
leading her horse. Boldwood fetched his from a tree to   25
which he had tied it.

Oak was so busy watching them while still shearing a
sheep, that he cut the animal, and it jumped. Bathsheba
at once went to the sheep and saw the blood. Teasingly,
she criticized Gabriel for his carelessness. Oak blamed   30
Bathsheba for the mistake, because, he thought, she had

hurt him even more than he had hurt the sheep, but he hid his feelings.

'Bottle!' he shouted, and Cain quickly brought him the medicine to put on the wound.

Then Bathsheba said to Oak, 'I'm going to see Mr Boldwood's sheep now. Take my place here, Gabriel, and be careful to make sure the men do their work properly.'

Then she rode away with Boldwood.

'That means that they're going to marry,' one of the workers said.

'Perhaps the time has come for it,' said another. 'I believe Farmer Boldwood kissed her behind the hedge at the sheep washing.'

'That's a lie!' said Gabriel.

'How do you know?'

'Because she told me.'

The other men went on talking, and Oak went on shearing without saying another word. He realized that his scolding of Bathsheba had been a mistake. She had not been playing tricks on Boldwood, but on him, Gabriel Oak, by claiming that she had not been serious about Boldwood. He now believed that the other men were right, and that she would accept Boldwood's offer that same day.

A scene of passion

That evening all the workers were going to have a supper together after the end of the shearing. A long table was set up partly in the house by an open window, but most of it was outside on the grass. Bathsheba sat at the end that was in the house, looking particularly pretty.

She had just asked Gabriel to sit at the other end of the long table opposite her, which he did very happily, when Farmer Boldwood arrived. He went to Bathsheba and apologized for being late, so it was clear that he had been invited. He was wearing much brighter clothes than he usually did.

Bathsheba asked Gabriel to move, so that Mr Boldwood could sit at the other end of the table.

The eating and drinking began, and went on for a long time, and then there were songs until long after the sun had gone down.

Then suddenly Gabriel noticed that Farmer Boldwood was not in his chair, and while he was thinking about this, Liddy lit some candles in the room at the opposite end of the table. Gabriel saw that Boldwood had gone inside the house, and was now sitting next to Bathsheba.

The men now wanted her to sing for them, and she asked Gabriel to play his flute while she sang. The song she chose was about a soldier who got a girl to marry him by his clever talk. Many years later, people remembered that song.

When her song was finished, Bathsheba said, 'Good night' to all her workers, and the window shutters were closed so that no one could see in. Boldwood remained in the room with Bathsheba, and soon afterwards a scene of passion unfolded itself.

Miss Everdene's eyes soon grew bright with the excitement of a triumph — though it was a triumph that she had expected rather than wanted. She was standing behind a low chair, from which she had just risen, and

Boldwood was kneeling on it, holding her hand in both his own. A usually very dignified man, he had changed completely, and this took away much of the pleasure that Bathsheba had from the proof that he loved her so deeply.

5 'I will try to love you,' she said to him in a trembling voice, which was very different from her usual confidence in herself. 'If I can believe that I shall be a good wife to you, I shall be willing to marry you. But I don't want to promise anything tonight. Please wait a few weeks till I
10 can see things more clearly.'

'But you think that then ..?'

'I have every reason to hope at the end of the five or six weeks between now and harvest, when you say you are going to be away from home, that I shall be able to
15 make that promise,' she said firmly. 'But remember this clearly: I don't promise anything yet.'

'That is enough. I do not ask for more. And now, Miss Everdene, good night!'

'Good night,' she answered in a kind — almost a tender
20 — voice, and he left with a happy smile.

Bathsheba knew more of his character now. He had opened his heart to her completely. She very much regretted what she had done to this man, and was struggling to put things right, without thinking whether
25 her sin quite deserved the punishment she was about to give herself. She was beginning to find a fearful joy in the situation. It is wonderful how easily even the most hesitant women sometimes begin to enjoy quite frightening things when they are linked to some social triumph.

30 **Hooked together**

One of the duties that Bathsheba had taken on when she dismissed the bailiff was that of going round the farm before going to bed to see that everything was all right. Gabriel usually went ahead of her to protect her, but in
35 most cases she did not know that he was doing this.

As the best way to check things is to do it secretly, she usually carried a dark lantern, so that she could turn the light on only when she wanted to see something. She thought that it was quite safe to do this.

The night of the shearing supper, she was walking along a path under some trees when she thought she heard footsteps. A figure appeared in the darkness, and just as the person passed her, something caught the edge of her skirt and seemed to fix it to the ground.

'Sorry,' a man's voice said. 'Have I hurt you, friend?'

'No,' said Bathsheba, trying to move away.

'We have got hooked together somehow, I think.'

'Yes.'

'Are you a woman?'

'Yes.'

'Is that a dark lantern you are holding?'

'Yes.'

'If you will allow me, I'll open it and set you free.'

A hand took the lantern and opened it. Bathsheba had been expecting to see some dangerous man in dark clothes, so she was highly relieved to notice that the man to whom she was hooked was a soldier in a red coat. His spur had caught in the edge of her dress. The man saw her face.

'I'll get it off in a moment, miss,' he said.

'Oh, no, I can do it, thank you,' she answered quickly, and bent down to free herself. But it was not easy. The cloth was wound round the spur in a complicated way.

The man bent down, too, now, and the light from the lantern shone on both their faces.

He looked hard into her eyes when she raised them for a moment, and she quickly looked down again,

because his eyes were too strong to be stared at so directly
by her own. But she had noticed that he was young, and
that he had a sergeant's stripes on his sleeve.

'I'm sorry,' he said, 'but I shall have to cut your dress
if you are in a hurry.'

'Yes, please do,' she answered helplessly.

'It wouldn't be necessary if you could wait a moment.'
He untied a thread from his spur, and touched her hand,
either accidentally or on purpose. Bathsheba felt angry
without knowing quite why.

The man continued with the threads, but it seemed to
go on for a very long time. She looked at him again.

'Thank you for the sight of such a beautiful face,' the
young sergeant said suddenly.

She was embarrassed, and blushed. 'I didn't show it
willingly,' she answered coldly and with as much dignity
as she could find in her position as a prisoner.

'Your truthfulness makes me like you all the more,
miss,' he said.

'Oh, how can you insult me so? I wish you had never
shown yourself to me by coming here.' She pulled again,
and threads from her dress began to break.

'Look at that!' she continued. 'You've been making it
worse intentionally, in order to keep me here.'

'I don't think so,' the sergeant answered merrily.

'You have!' she said angrily. 'Now let me do it.'

'Certainly, miss. I am thankful for beauty, even when it
is thrown to me like a bone to a dog.'

The handsome stranger

Bathsheba was wondering whether to pull hard, at the
risk of pulling her skirt right off. The thought was too
terrible. She was still wearing her best dress, which she
had put on for the supper, and what woman in
Bathsheba's position would have risked ruining such a
dress just to escape from a handsome soldier?

'Who are you?' she asked the man.

'Sergeant Troy. I'm on leave from my regiment … There, you're free now. I wish it had been the knot of knots, which cannot be untied.' He meant marriage.

This was worse and worse. She got up immediately, and so did he. How could she get away from him in a dignified way — that was her difficulty now. She moved off slowly until she could not see his red coat any more.

'Ah, Beauty, goodbye,' he said.

She said nothing, but when she was twenty or thirty yards away, she began to run.

When she got to the house, she said to Liddy, 'Is there a soldier staying in the village? A sergeant who is rather like a gentleman?'

'Well, it might be Sergeant Troy. He may have come home on leave.'

'What kind of a man is this Sergeant Troy?'

'He's very clever, but he chases the girls terribly! He's a doctor's son, but they say his real father was a lord.'

Bathsheba went to bed and thought about Sergeant Troy. How could a cheerful woman be offended for long by such a man?

There are times when a girl like Bathsheba is willing to accept a lot of unusual behaviour. This happens when she wants to be praised, which is often; when she wants a strong-minded man, which is sometimes; and when she wants no nonsense, which is seldom. At this moment the first of these three feelings was the strongest in her, with a little of the second, too. What made the sensation even more exciting was that the man was a handsome stranger with an interesting past.

Finally she decided that perhaps it had been she who was wrong by running away like that from a man who had only been both polite and kind to her. Clearly, she did not think that his praise of her was an insult now. Boldwood had made a terrible mistake by never telling her that she was beautiful.

SERGEANT TROY'S TRIUMPH

Pleasing words

Sergeant Troy was a man who thought only about the present. He never considered the past, or the future. For this reason, he was never disappointed, because one is
5 disappointed only if one is hoping for something in the future, and it does not happen.

He was usually truthful to men, but to women he lied all the time. He often sinned, but never in an ugly way, so many people smiled at his immoral behaviour, even
10 while they disapproved. Above all, he was wonderful at flattering women. He knew that talking about love and beauty did not have to be reasonable, it just had to be clever.

He used to say to anyone who listened that there were
15 only two ways of treating women: telling them how wonderful they were, or cursing and swearing at them. There was no third way. 'If you treat them fairly,' he said, 'they will despise you.'

A week or two later, Troy appeared again on Bathsheba's farm for the hay-making. One afternoon Bathsheba was looking over the hedge watching the men as they worked, and she was very relieved to see that Boldwood was not there. Then she noticed a man in a bright red coat helping the others to load hay onto a cart. It was the sergeant.

As soon as Troy saw her, he stopped his work and came forward. Bathsheba was half angry and half embarrassed. She blushed, and fixed her eyes on the path that she was walking along.

'Ah, Miss Everdene,' said the sergeant, 'I had not realized that it was you I was speaking to the other night when we met. But if I had thought more carefully, I would have understood that the "Queen of the Corn Market", as everyone now calls you, could not have been any other woman. I come now to beg your pardon for speaking to you too boldly the other night as a stranger. Of course, I am not really a stranger to this place: I helped your uncle many times in these fields when I was a boy. I have been doing the same for you today.'

'I suppose that I must thank you for that,' Bathsheba answered in a voice that showed no interest.

'No, you do not need to do that if you do not wish to,' the sergeant answered, but he looked hurt and sad.

'I am glad that it is not necessary.'

'Could I ask why?'

'Because I really don't want to have to thank you for anything.'

'I am afraid that my tongue has done damage that my heart will never mend. What bad luck for telling a woman honestly that she is beautiful!'

'There are some kinds of talk that I need less than help on my farm. I would be happier not to have you here.'

'And I would prefer to have curses from you than kisses from any other woman, so I shall stay. I suppose that praise can be rude, and I may have been guilty of that. But there is also treatment that is unjust, and you may have been guilty of that.'

'I don't allow strangers to be bold and rude to me — or even to praise me,' answered Bathsheba, turning away.

'Ah, what offends you is not what I said, but how I said it. But I have the satisfaction of knowing that my words, whether pleasing or not, were true.'

'Oh, you are just pretending,' Bathsheba said, laughing in spite of herself at his clever talk. 'Why couldn't you have passed me by that evening without saying anything?'

'Because half the pleasure of a feeling comes from being able to express it immediately.'

'How long have you suffered from such strong feelings then?'

'Since I was big enough to know the difference between beauty and ugliness.'

'I hope that you know as much about morals as you seem to know about pretty faces.'

'I am sure I would have been a much more moral man if all you pretty women had not misled me.'

Bathsheba moved away to hide the smile that was coming to her face.

Troy followed. 'But — Miss Everdene — you do forgive me, don't you?'

'Hardly.'

'Why?'

'You say such things.'

'I said you were beautiful, and I'll go on saying so! You are the most beautiful woman I've ever seen!'

'Don't — don't — I won't listen to you.' She was half worried by his words, and half wanting to hear more.

'But it is true, isn't it?'

'No,' she whispered. 'I do not think that I am really so beautiful.'

'That is because of your modesty. But surely everybody must have told you.'

'Not directly,' Bathsheba went on. That was a mistake; she was allowing herself to be drawn even further into a conversation that she had planned to avoid.

'But you know that they think so.'

'No — well, I certainly heard Liddy say they do, but ...'

The careless sergeant knew what these words meant. Bathsheba, without knowing it, had admitted her vanity. That was the turning point of the whole affair. A seed had been planted in her mind. The sergeant had only to wait for time and nature to do their work on her, and she would be his.

'Don't speak to me like that again!'

'I will risk saying something that may upset you now,' the sergeant went on, 'and that is that your beauty may do more harm than good. The reason I think that is because, on average, one man probably falls in love with one ordinary woman. They marry, and have a happy life together. But a hundred men fall in love with a woman like you, and only one of them can marry you. So, ninety-nine other men, and ninety-nine women will all lead unhappy lives.'

'If you can fight half as well as you can talk, you must be a wonderful soldier!' answered Bathsheba. Then she realized the mistake she had made, and added, hastily, 'But don't think that your words give me any pleasure.'

'I am not so stupid as to think that. But I had hoped that the kindness of your heart would have stopped you from judging me so coldly this morning, when I have been working so hard for you.'

'Well, perhaps you did not intend to be rude, and I do thank you for helping. But don't speak to me like that again — or in any way, unless I speak to you first.'

'Oh, Miss Bathsheba, that is too hard! Then you will never speak to me again, because I shan't be here long. I have to go back to my regiment.'

'When are you going?' Bathsheba asked with some interest.

'In a month.'

'If you're really interested in such nonsense, then I don't mind speaking to you,' answered Bathsheba, but her voice was doubting and hesitant.

'That's unfair. You know nothing of what a man feels like when he is deeply in love with a woman, and cannot think, hear or look in any direction without suffering to the depths of his heart.'

'Oh, you are pretending again,' she said, shaking her head. 'You only saw me for a few moments the other night.'

'That makes no difference. Lightning only has to strike once.'

'I won't listen to you any longer. I wish I knew what time it was. I'm going. I've wasted enough time already.'

The watch

The sergeant looked at his watch and told Bathsheba what the time was. 'Haven't you got a watch, miss?' he asked.

'Mine is broken. I'm going to get a new one soon.'

'No, you must take this one as a present from me, Miss Everdene.'

And before she knew what the man intended to do, a heavy gold watch was placed in her hand.

'It is an unusually good one for a man like me to possess,' he said quietly. 'Look.'

Inside the back of the watch was the crest of a wealthy family.

'That is the crest of the Earls of Severn. It belonged to the last lord, and was given to my mother's husband, a medical man, until I reached the age of twenty-one. It was the only thing I got from him. Now it's yours.'

'But Sergeant Troy — I can't take this!' she exclaimed, her eyes round with surprise.

She held the watch out to him, but he stepped back so as not to receive it. She went forward, and he continued to go backwards.

'Keep it,' he said. 'The fact that you have it will make it worth ten times as much to me.'

'But I really can't take it!' Bathsheba answered in a very worried voice. 'You can't give me your dead father's watch!'

'I loved my father, but I love you more, so I can do it.'

Bathsheba was now so worried that she really looked extraordinarily beautiful. Troy was struck dumb by the sight, and quite surprised that she was really as lovely as he had pretended to think of her before.

'My workers can see me following you around, and they are wondering what is happening — oh, this is too dreadful!' Bathsheba went on. She knew nothing of the change that was coming over Troy.

'I did not really want you to have it at first, because it was my only sign of having come from a noble family, but now — honestly — I want you to keep it.'

'No, no — I have reasons for not wanting it which I cannot explain.'

'All right then,' he said and took the watch back at last. 'I must go now. Will you speak to me during these few weeks that I shall be here?'

'Yes, I will … But I don't know if I will. Oh, why did you come and disturb me like this?'

'Perhaps I have caught myself in the trap I was setting for someone else.'

Troy returned to the other workers in the fields, but Bathsheba could not face them now. Her heart was racing. She was hot, excited, and unable to think clearly. As she returned home, she whispered to herself, 'Oh, what have I done — what does it mean? I wish I knew how much of it was true!'

The swordsman

A few days later, Troy helped Bathsheba again. Some bees had flown away from their hives. Everyone else was out getting the hay in, so Bathsheba decided to try to catch them herself. One swarm had settled at the top of a tree. She had fetched a ladder, which she set against the tree. She was just starting to climb up when she heard a voice that was beginning to have a strange power over her.

'Miss Everdene, let me help you.'

Quickly she climbed down, holding her skirt tight round her legs. She passed her hat, veil and gloves over to Troy. When he had put them on, he looked so funny that she laughed. Another part of the barrier of formal manners between them had been broken.

After he had brought the swarm down and returned it to its hive, he said, 'Really, this makes one's arm ache. It's worse than a week of exercise with a sword. Will you please help me take these things off? I can hardly breathe in them.'

'I've never seen sword-exercise,' she said while she was taking the veil and other things off him.

'Would you like to?'

'Yes, I would like it very much.'

At eight o'clock that evening, Bathsheba met Troy a little way outside Weatherbury village. When he saw her coming, he took out a sword and raised it. It flashed in the last of the day's sunlight.

'Now,' he said, 'you will be my enemy, except that I shall miss you every time by a fraction of an inch. Be very careful not to move, even if you feel frightened.'

Bathsheba was beginning to enjoy the sense of danger. She stood in front of Troy without moving while his sword flashed past her, once on one side and then once on the other side. She did not move.

Before making any more moves he said, 'Now, if you are afraid, I can't go on. But I can promise you that I will not touch you once.'

'I'm not afraid.'

The sword exercise began. Bathsheba felt the air disturbed by the blade of the sword as it passed her again and again.

Then Troy stopped. He said, 'There's a piece of your hair that's hanging loose. I'm going to tidy it for you.'

The sword flashed, and the piece of hair fell to the ground.

'You're a brave woman!' Troy said. 'You didn't move an inch. That's wonderful in a woman! And now I'm going to kill that insect on you. Don't move!'   5

She saw the point of the sword flash towards her chest, and seem to enter it. She closed her eyes, sure that she had been killed. But she felt nothing, and opened them again.

The insect was stuck on the point of the sword.   10

'I must leave you now,' said Troy softly. 'And I'll take this, if you let me, to remember you by.' He picked up the piece of hair that he had cut off and put it carefully in his pocket. She felt that she was completely in his power now. He came closer and closer, and then turned   15 quickly, and disappeared among the bushes.

In that short moment, the blood had come beating into her face, and filled her with feelings that quite prevented her from thinking. It also made her weep a great stream of tears. She felt like someone who had sinned deeply.   20 The reason was that Troy's mouth had dipped gently onto hers as he passed. He had kissed her.

The ache in her heart

Bathsheba's reason was too strong to be completely ruled by her feelings as a woman; and these were too strong to   25 allow her to use her reason in the best way, so she was a mixture of the sensible and the foolish. She could believe flattery that she knew to be false, and not believe criticism that she knew to be true.

She loved Troy in a way that only strong women can love when they give up their strength. One problem was that she had never been in such a position before, and therefore had no experience of how to deal with it.

The bad side of Troy's character was hidden, while his attractions were on the surface. Oak was the opposite: his weaknesses could be seen clearly, while his virtues were hidden.

Oak could see that Bathsheba was getting into a dangerous situation with Troy. This made him sadder than the fact that she did not love him.

He spoke to her one evening about his worries, and pleaded with her to be more careful. However, his words only upset Bathsheba, and made her feel even more sad and confused.

Soon after this, Troy said he was going away to the city of Bath for two days, to visit friends. When he had gone, Bathsheba wrote a letter to Boldwood, telling him that she could not marry him. The letter could not go until the next day, but she wanted to get it off her hands, so she went to find one of the women in the kitchen to give it to her. She stopped outside the door. She could hear Liddy and some of the other women talking about her and Troy.

This made Bathsheba very angry. She shouted at Liddy. Liddy in her turn became angry, and said she no longer wanted to work for Bathsheba. This made Bathsheba realize just how badly her love for Troy was affecting her judgement.

'No, no, Liddy, you must stay!' she begged. 'I don't know what I'm doing since this ache in my heart began.'

Liddy herself now saw that she had spoken too hastily. 'I won't leave you,' she said, beginning to cry, and suddenly she kissed Bathsheba on the lips.

MARRIED!

Powerful feelings

The next evening, Bathsheba decided to go to Upper Mellstock to stay with Liddy for a day or two. She had only walked about a mile down the road when she saw Boldwood coming slowly towards her. Clearly he was on his way to the farm, to talk to her about her letter.

When they met, Bathsheba was the first to speak.

'Oh, it's you, Mr Boldwood,' she said. Her face went a guilty red.

For a long time Boldwood said nothing, but his eyes showed how he was feeling. Bathsheba looked away, and he said, 'Are you afraid of me then?'

'Why do you say that?'

'I thought you looked afraid. And it surprised me, because my feeling for you is quite different.'

Bathsheba looked at him and waited.

'You know how I feel,' Boldwood continued slowly.

'I wish you didn't,' Bathsheba whispered. She did not know how to get out of this situation. She began to move on, but Boldwood followed her, looking miserable.

'Oh, Bathsheba, have pity on me!' he pleaded. 'Don't throw me off now!'

'How can I throw you off? I never had you.'

'But it was you who sent me your valentine.'

'That was just a childish game. I have bitterly regretted it, and I pity you deeply. I was wrong to do what I did, but you do not have to punish me so cruelly. Can't you forgive me and forget about the whole thing?'

'Oh, Miss Everdene, you are not the cold woman you are pretending to be. You have a burning heart like mine, but it has turned onto a new direction. I know where.'

Bathsheba's heart had been beating fast, but now it beat even faster. Boldwood was going to speak of Troy. So he knew!

'Why could Sergeant Troy not leave you alone?' he asked fiercely. 'If he had not come, you would have agreed to marry me, wouldn't you?'

Bathsheba was too honest not to whisper, 'Yes.'

'Now everyone is laughing at me. Well, go and marry your new man then — go on!'

His anger frightened her. She said, 'Please don't speak to me like that! Everyone is finding fault with me now. I have no one else to fight my battles for me, but no sympathy or mercy is shown.'

'He has kissed you, hasn't he?'

'Leave me, sir! Let me go on!' Bathsheba answered with trembling cheeks.

'He has kissed you, hasn't he?'

'Yes, he has,' she answered slowly, and, in spite of her fear, bravely. 'I'm not ashamed to speak the truth.'

'Then I curse him!' Boldwood whispered, deeply angry. 'A time will come when he'll be sorry for that — and then he'll ache, and wish, and curse as I do now!'

'Don't wish an evil fate for him!' Bathsheba begged miserably. 'Be kind to him, sir, because I truly love him!'

'I'll punish him. I'll whip him!' Then suddenly he began to speak more quietly. 'Bathsheba, my dear, pardon me. I've been blaming you and threatening you, when he's the one who's to blame. He stole your heart with his lies and clever talk!'

With this, he left. Bathsheba covered her face with her hands, and tried to calm down. She could not understand how a quiet man like Mr Boldwood could have such powerful feelings. It filled her with terror.

Bathsheba knew that her lover was coming back to Weatherbury in the next day or two, and this made Boldwood's threats all the more frightening. She walked up and down, weeping quietly.

A horse thief

That night, Maryann suddenly woke. She thought she had
heard someone outside the house. She got up and went
to the window. Pushing open the shutters, she looked out
and saw a figure moving around silently in the darkness.   5
It went up to a horse, caught it and took it to the corner
of the field, where there was a small carriage. A few
minutes later, Maryann heard the carriage driving away.

Maryann had been afraid to shout out while the thief
was near, but now she dressed and ran to the nearest farm   10
worker's house. It belonged to Coggan.

Quickly she told him what had happened, and they ran
to Gabriel's house. They could still hear the horse and
carriage in the distance. Gabriel said, 'We must follow.'

'We haven't got a horse that's fast enough,' Coggan said.   15
'If only we had the two that are on the other side of the
hedge, we might do something.'

'Which two?'

'Mr Boldwood's.'

The two men got long pieces of rope, ran down to   20
Boldwood's fields, and caught the horses. They rode away
on them without saddles, and with only the ropes in their
mouths to guide them.

They rode off fast, stopping from time to time to listen,
and to look for tracks in the road. After the tracks had   25
gone some miles, they turned off towards the city of Bath.

'We shall catch him now,' Coggan said. 'There's a toll-
gate a mile ahead. I know the keeper there — he must
be the sleepiest gatekeeper between here and London.'

At the toll-gate   30

Soon they saw the white bars of the gate, and the carriage
in front of it. They rode up to it and shouted, 'Keep that
gate shut! He's stolen a horse!'

The man who collected the money said, 'Who?'

Gabriel looked at the driver of the carriage. It was Bathsheba. When she had heard his voice, she had turned her face away from the light, but Coggan saw her, too.

5 She hid her surprise and answered coolly, 'Well, Gabriel, where are you going?'

'We thought —' Gabriel began.

'I'm driving to Bath,' she said. 'Important business made it necessary for me to give up my visit to Liddy and go
10 off at once. Were you following me?'

'We thought that someone had stolen the horse.'

'How very foolish of you not to know that I had taken the horse and carriage! I tried to wake Maryann, but couldn't. Didn't you think that it might be me?'

15 'Why should we, miss?'

'Perhaps not. But those horses you have there. They can't be Farmer Boldwood's, can they? Oh, Gabriel, what have you been doing, bringing trouble on me like this?'

'But how could we know?' complained Coggan. 'And
20 ladies don't usually drive around at night.'

'I wrote in chalk on the door that I'd taken the horse and carriage.'

'But you must have known that we wouldn't see that till the morning, madam.'

'True,' she answered, and though she was angry at first, she realized that she could not really blame them for having done what they thought would help her. 'Well, thank you very much. And now please go home.'

She turned her head and drove off, and Gabriel and Coggan rode away in the opposite direction.

'Coggan,' said Gabriel, 'I think we should keep this night's work a secret.'

'I agree,' Coggan replied.

Bathsheba's plan

After her meeting with Boldwood, Bathsheba had decided there were only two solutions to her problems. One was to keep Troy away until Boldwood's anger had cooled. The other was to leave Troy completely.

After a time she thought the second of these choices would be best. Unfortunately, even though she fully understood Troy's real character, and realized that he might soon stop loving her, this did not make her love him any less. In fact it made her love him more.

A letter would not have got to him in time, so she had decided to go to Bath to see him. She wanted to make sure he did not come to Weatherbury. Also she wanted him to know why she had decided to break with him.

By then it was quite dark. The only thing to do was to give up the idea of staying with Liddy, go back home, and drive at once to Bath. It was a long way, even for a strong horse, and it was a very bold thing for a woman to do alone at night.

Her plan had been to see Troy the next morning, say goodbye to him, and dismiss him from her life. Then she could go on to Liddy at Upper Mellstock, and nobody would know that she had been to Bath at all.

A week passed without any news of Bathsheba. Then a letter came for Maryann. It said that the business that had taken her mistress to Bath still kept her there.

Another week passed. The harvest was going on in the
fields when Coggan saw a figure running towards them.
It was Cain Ball, who had been away for a few days.

'I've been in Bath,' he gasped after all his running. As
5 soon as he mentioned Bath, all the workers stopped and
listened.

'Yes, I've seen our mistress and a soldier walking
together. I think the soldier was Sergeant Troy. They went
and sat in a park. At first our mistress was crying, but
10 when they came out of the park, her eyes were shining.
I think our mistress and the soldier must be lovers.'

A business talk

That evening Bathsheba and Liddy returned to the farm.
Later Boldwood came. He knocked at the door. He told
15 Liddy that he had called to apologize for his ill temper.

Liddy went back in, and then came out again.

'My mistress cannot see you, sir,' she said.

The farmer immediately went away. He realized that
Bathsheba had not forgiven him.

20 On his way home, he saw a carriage. It stopped outside
a house, and a man in a red uniform got out. It was Troy.

'Sergeant Troy?' Boldwood called out.

'Yes.'

'I'm William Boldwood. I wish to speak to you.'
25 'What about?'

'About a woman whom you have treated badly.'

'Whether I have treated any woman badly or not, is no
business of yours,' said Troy, moving on.

Boldwood stood in front of him. 'You are going to talk
30 with me whether you like it or not,' he said.

Troy could hear the determination in Boldwood's voice.
He could see that he was a strong man, and that he had
a heavy stick in his hand, so he thought he had better be
polite.

35 'All right, I'll be happy to listen,' he said.

'Well, then, I know about you and Fanny Robin. You ought to marry her.'

'I suppose that I ought. In fact, I want to, but I cannot.'

'Why?'

'I am too poor.'

'Can we talk business?' Boldwood went on.

'All right.'

'Miss Everdene had agreed to marry me,' Boldwood continued, 'but you came and —'

'She had not agreed.'

'Well, almost agreed.'

'If I had not arrived, she might have agreed.'

'Not might — would certainly have agreed. And if you hadn't met her, you might have married Fanny. Well, there's too much difference in social position between you and Miss Everdene. She is the tenant of a large farm, and you are just an ordinary soldier; it is impossible for you to think of marrying her. So all I ask is that you won't see her any more. I'll pay you for it. I'll give you fifty pounds now, and I'll give Fanny another fifty, and she shall have 500 on her wedding day.'

'I like Fanny best,' said Troy, 'and I accept your offer.'

Just then light footsteps were heard on the path.

'It's she,' Troy said. 'I must go and meet her.'

'She — who?'

'Bathsheba.'

'Bathsheba? Out alone at this time of night?' said Boldwood, very surprised.

'She was expecting me tonight — and now I must say goodbye to her, as you wish.'

'I don't see any reason for you to speak to her.'

'It can't do any harm. You'll hear everything I say to her. And remember this: if she doesn't know what's happened to me, she'll spend more time worrying about me than if I tell her that I'm going to leave her.'

As the footsteps came nearer, Troy whistled like a bird.

'Frank, dearest,' said Bathsheba's voice. 'Is that you?'

'Yes,' Troy answered.

'Oh, God!' said Boldwood to himself, quietly.

'I've sent all the women out, so nobody will know about your visit,' said Bathsheba.

5   'Good,' said Troy, 'but I'd better go and get my bag. I'll be at your house in ten minutes.'

The newspaper announcement

Bathsheba went away — she had not seen Boldwood standing there. Boldwood was terribly shocked. He stared 10 at Troy in astonishment.

'You see how much she loves me. Shall I tell her that I can't marry her?' Troy said.

'No — no — wait,' Boldwood whispered. He was finding it difficult to speak.

15 'Now you see my problem,' said Troy. 'I can't marry them both. And I have two reasons for choosing Fanny. First I like her best, and second you will pay me —'

At that moment Boldwood seized him by the neck. Troy was quite unprepared for this.

'If you hurt me, you will be hurting the woman you love,' he managed to gasp.

Boldwood let him go. 'By Heaven,' he said, 'I'd like to kill you!'

'But if you do, that will destroy Bathsheba.'

'It will save her.'

'Oh, how can she be saved now unless I marry her? It would be a mistake to kill me, wouldn't it?'

'Yes.'

'It would be better to kill yourself.'

'Much better. Marry her, Troy. She must love you more deeply than I had thought.'

'But Bathsheba has a strong will and a hot temper. She will treat me like a slave. I could do anything with poor Fanny.'

'Please, Troy,' answered Boldwood, 'please be good to Bathsheba. Marry her. I'll help you. I'll give you the 500 pounds when you marry her.'

'Will you give me some more money now, too?'

'Yes, I haven't brought much, but you can have it. But you must sign a paper —'

'I'll sign when I have received payment in full. But she must never know about it.'

'All right.'

They walked together to Bathsheba's house. At the door, Troy said, 'Wait here a moment.' He went in.

Two minutes later Troy came back, carrying a candle. He handed Boldwood a newspaper, pointing to one place on the page.

Boldwood read it. It was the announcement of the wedding of Francis Troy to Bathsheba Everdene in Bath on the 17th of that month.

Troy laughed at Boldwood's confusion. 'I might be bad,' he said, 'but I don't buy and sell women. Fanny left me a long time ago. I have tried to find her, but without success. You say you love Bathsheba, but you at once believed that she was behaving immorally with me. Now that I've taught you a lesson, take your money back.'

'I will not!' Boldwood answered angrily.

'Well, I won't have it,' said Troy. He threw the money into the road.

'I'll punish you!' Boldwood said, shaking his fist at him.

Troy laughed again before closing and locking the door.

All that night Boldwood walked over the hills and through the valleys of Weatherbury like an unhappy ghost.

8

TROUBLE WITH TROY

The new master

Early the next morning Gabriel Oak and Coggan were
going to the fields when they saw the shutters of
Bathsheba's bedroom window being pushed open. A
5 handsome man looked out. It was Sergeant Troy. Coggan
said quietly, 'She has married him!'

Gabriel's face turned white. He turned his back, and
said nothing. For the past week Oak had suspected that
Bathsheba and Troy had married, and this made him feel
10 terribly sad.

The two men moved on again, but Troy shouted to
them cheerfully from the window:

'Good morning, friends!'

Coggan replied, and then said to Gabriel, 'Go on, say
15 good morning. It won't mean anything.'

'Good morning, Sergeant,' Gabriel said coldly.

'Coggan, do you know if there has been any madness
in Mr Boldwood's family?' Troy asked.

'I once heard that an uncle of his was slightly insane.'

20 'Well, we'll talk about it later,' Troy answered. 'I just
wanted to say I hope we'll remain friends as usual. Here's
two shillings for you both to buy yourselves a drink with.'

He threw the money down. Gabriel turned away
angrily, but Coggan picked it up.

25 'You keep it,' Gabriel said to Coggan. 'I won't accept
any gifts from him!'

'Be careful what you say,' Coggan replied. 'If he's
married her, he'll be our master here.'

'Perhaps you're right, but if I can only keep my job here
30 by being polite to him, I'll go.'

A horseman now approached, and soon they saw that it was Mr Boldwood. They greeted him politely, and he rode on.

'I wonder what Troy meant by that question,' Coggan said.

The corn ricks

One night in August, at the end of the harvest, Oak was in the farmyard looking at eight corn ricks. He was worried, because they were not covered, and he felt that heavy rain was coming. This was the night that Troy, who had now left his regiment and was behaving as the master of the farm, had chosen for the harvest-supper and dance.

Oak decided to talk to Troy about the weather and the corn ricks. He went to the barn where the party was going on. Inside it was noisy and very crowded. He sent Troy a message, telling him that it was going to rain heavily soon, and that something must be done to protect the corn.

The messenger came back. 'Mr Troy says that it isn't going to rain, and he cannot stop and talk to you about such unimportant things,' he told Gabriel.

As Oak was about to leave, Troy stood up to speak to everyone. 'Friends,' he said, 'this party is not only for the harvest. It is also to celebrate a wedding. I have ordered some bottles of brandy, and kettles of hot water so that you can all drink to your mistress and me.'

Bathsheba put her hand on his arm. 'Don't give it to them, please, Frank,' she begged. 'They are not used to brandy — it is too strong for them. They've already had enough to drink.'

'Yes, we don't want any more,' some of the guests said.

'Nonsense!' answered Troy. 'Friends, we'll send the women home, and then have a really good party. If any of the men refuse, then I don't want them working on this farm. They can work for someone else in future.'

Bathsheba left the barn angrily, followed by all the women and children.

Oak stayed for a while, but then returned to the farmyard. He knew that if the corn ricks got very wet, the corn would be valueless, and Bathsheba would lose all her profit from that year's harvest. Lightning was flashing fiercely in the distance. It would not be long before it began to rain.

He had to get the corn ricks covered, so he went back to see if he could find anyone to help him. By that time all was quiet in the barn. He thought everybody had gone home, but he saw a light, so he looked in. Everywhere men were lying about, on chairs, over tables or on the floor. They were all asleep. Troy was in the middle of them. Gabriel also noticed Coggan, lying on his back with his mouth wide open.

Gabriel realized that, if the corn was going to be saved, he would have to do it himself. He put out any candles that were still alight, in case the barn caught fire, and then went out again into the darkness.

He found four large covers and used them to cover two of the ricks. After that there were no more covers, so he took a pitchfork, and began placing straw sheaves on top of the other ricks to protect them. But before he could finish the work, a rush of air told him that the storm had arrived.

Bathsheba helps

Suddenly a bright flash of blue light struck very near him. His pitchfork was made of metal, so there was a danger that the lightning would strike it. He found a chain, and hung it from the top of a rick to the ground some distance away from where he was working. It would act as a conductor and keep the lightning away from him.

The next flash showed a woman standing in the yard.

'Is that you, madam?' Gabriel called out.

'Oh, Gabriel,' Bathsheba replied, 'the storm woke me, and I thought of the corn. I can't find my husband anywhere.'

'He isn't here. He's asleep in the barn.'

'He promised to look after the ricks, but I can see that he has done nothing. Can I help?'

'You can bring me some more sheaves of straw, madam, if you aren't afraid of climbing up the ladder in the dark. We must work fast. Every moment is precious now.'

Bathsheba at once began to lift the heavy sheaves up to Gabriel. She carried up one after another. There was no rain yet, but the lightning blazed and the thunder roared very fiercely. A particularly bright flash of lightning came, and a deafening crash of thunder. It terrified Bathsheba. Gabriel caught her arm to stop her falling. The lightning had struck the chain that Gabriel had hung on the corn rick, and gone harmlessly into the ground. Immediately afterwards, another flash of lightning hit a tree and tore it right down the middle.

'We had better go down' Gabriel said.

Bathsheba was afraid, and in her fear she began to breathe quickly, but she did not panic. She climbed down the ladder, and Gabriel followed. They waited for some time at the foot of the rick, until all was quiet.

'The storm seems to have passed,' Gabriel said. 'I'll go up again.'

'Oh, Gabriel, you're kinder than I deserve!'

He climbed to the top of a rick, and she followed, but without a sheaf.

'Gabriel,' she said, 'when I went to Bath that night, I suppose you thought I went there because I wanted to be married.'

'I did in the end, mistress,' he said, 'but not at first.'

'I care for your good opinion, and I want to explain something. When I went to Bath that night, it was to tell Mr Troy that I could not marry him. It was because of things that happened after I got there that we married.

When I went to see Mr Troy, he told me that he had just
met a woman who was more beautiful than I was, and
that unless I at once became his … I was so worried and
jealous that I married him! It was my own wish: it wasn't
5   his fault. And now I don't want you ever to say anything
more on this subject.'

She continued to bring sheaves up until Gabriel, seeing
that she was tired, said to her gently, 'Go home. I can
finish the rest alone.'

10   'If I'm useless, I'll go.'

'You aren't useless, but I'd be happier if you went and
rested. You've done well.'

'And you've done better!' she answered gratefully.
'Thank you a thousand times, Gabriel, for your loyalty.'

15   He went on working, thinking about Bathsheba, till he
felt the wind change direction — a signal for the rain that
would soon come.

It was now five o'clock in the morning. The wind blew
more strongly, and some of the sheaves on top of the
20   ricks fell off, so that Gabriel had to put them back. The
rain began to fall hard.

Suddenly he remembered how, eight months before, he
had been fighting a fire here instead of rain — and,
hopelessly, for the love of the same woman.

25   He finished his work on the ricks at seven. As he moved
off, he heard sounds from the barn.
One man after another came out,
looking ashamed and walking
with some difficulty. Only the
first, who wore a red coat,
looked cheerful.

As Oak was walking home, he met Boldwood. He, too, was walking along slowly. They exchanged greetings.

'Are your ricks covered, sir?' Oak asked.

'No. I forgot about them.'

Oak was surprised. A few months before such a thing   5
would never have happened on Boldwood's farm.

The stranger

One Saturday evening, two months later, Bathsheba and Troy were coming home from Casterbridge market in a small carriage. She was sitting on one of the seats, and   10
Troy was walking beside the horse as they climbed a steep hill.

'Yes, my love,' Troy was saying, 'if this terrible rain hadn't come, I'd have won a 200-pound bet at the races.'

'And actually you've lost 100 pounds already by this   15
dreadful horse racing. Oh, Frank, it's cruel and foolish of you to use my money in this way. We shall have to leave the farm, and that will be the end of it.'

'Nonsense!'

'But you'll promise not to go to the next race meeting,   20
won't you?'

'I don't see why I should. I was thinking of taking you.'

'Never, never!'

'But it doesn't make any difference whether I go there or not. I make my bets before the races. You're being a   25
fool. I used to like you for you boldness, but now you've lost all that. If I'd known that you were going to become so weak and silly, I wouldn't have —'

Bathsheba looked angry for a moment, but then she looked straight ahead without saying another word.   30

A woman appeared at the top of the hill. When the carriage reached her, Troy got ready to climb into it, but at that moment the stranger spoke.

'Please, sir,' she said to Troy, 'do you know at what time the Casterbridge workhouse closes?'   35

Troy was very surprised to hear that voice, but he had his back to the woman and did not turn round. He answered slowly, 'I don't know.'

As soon as the woman heard his voice, she recognized Troy. At once her face showed a mixture of happiness and pain. She gave a terrible cry, and fell down. 'Oh, the poor girl!' exclaimed Bathsheba, beginning to get down from the carriage.

'Stay where you are and look after the horse!' ordered Troy. 'Go on now — I'll stay here and help her.'

'But I —'

'Do what I tell you!' The carriage moved on.

'How ever did you come here?' said Troy in a gentle but hurried voice as he lifted the woman up. 'I thought you were far away, or dead! Why didn't you write to me?'

'I was afraid to.'

'Have you any money?'

'None.'

'Well, here's all that I have left. Good Heavens — I wish I had more to give you. Where are you staying tonight? Casterbridge workhouse?'

'Yes. I am so poor there is nowhere else to go.'

'That is an awful place, but I can't do anything better for you, unfortunately. Listen. Just go there for tonight and tomorrow, but on Monday morning, meet me at Grey's Bridge at ten. I'll bring all the money I can get. Then I'll find you a place to live, dear. Goodbye till then!'

Troy went back to the carriage, got straight in and drove on.

'Who was that woman?' Bathsheba asked, looking hard at Troy's face.

'No one important,' he said. 'I met her once or twice before, but I don't know her name.'

'I think you do.'

'Think what you like,' he answered shortly.

Struggling through the night

The woman walked on in the dark night, until at last she could hardly put one foot in front of the other. She went into a field and lay down under some hay to sleep.

She woke an hour later, and could see the lights of Casterbridge in the distance.

'I wish I could get there,' she said, 'and meet him the day after tomorrow. But I may be dead by then.'

She got up and walked on slowly, and then she was tired again. She found two sticks, and used them to lean on as she continued her slow walk. Suddenly she saw something moving in front of her. It was a big black dog. It came up to her and licked her cheek. The animal was homeless like herself, and seemed to want company, so she put her arms round its shoulders and encouraged it to go forward. In that way, she had half her weight on the dog as she moved along.

Sometimes she wanted to stop, and then the dog, which seemed to understand how weak she was, eagerly pulled her on. At last they reached the gates of a big dark building. The woman raised herself as high as she could on her knees, and pulled a handle to ring the bell.

It was nearly six o'clock in the morning, and sounds were coming from inside the building. A man came to the door, and went back to get two women. Then they carried the figure that lay on the ground inside.

'There's a dog out there,' the woman whispered weakly. 'It helped me.'

'I threw a stone at it, and it went away,' said the man.

THE END OF A UNION

Suspicion

The next day was Sunday. In the evening Troy asked Bathsheba if she would let him have twenty pounds. He would not tell her why he wanted it. They began to
5 quarrel, but Bathsheba quickly gave in and let him have the money.

Troy looked at his watch, and for some reason, opened the back. Inside was a small ring of yellow hair. Bathsheba saw it, and immediately wanted to know whose hair it
10 was.

'It's the hair of a young woman I knew before I met you,' Troy explained.

'What's her name?'

'I can't tell you. Now, Bathsheba, don't be so jealous.'
15 Bathsheba was bitter now. 'When I married you, your life was dearer to me than my own; and now you just despise me. You'll burn that hair now, Frank, won't you?'

He pretended that he had not heard her. 'If you are now sorry that you married me, then so am I.'
20 'I'm only sorry you don't love me more than any other woman,' she said. 'But you already love someone more than you love me, don't you?'

'I don't know. Why do you say that?'

'Because you keep that lock of hair in the back of your
25 watch.'

'Until today I hadn't looked at it for months.'

'And then there was that woman that we met in the road yesterday.'

'It was that meeting that reminded me of the hair.'
30 'Is it hers, then?'

'Yes. Now you know, and I hope you are satisfied.'

'Once I felt that I could only be happy if my husband loved me deeply. Now I must be happy with anything that is not absolute cruelty.'

'Stop being so silly!' Troy said angrily, and walked out of the room.

Understanding

The next morning, Bathsheba got up earlier than usual, and rode round her farm as she always did. She thought of going to talk to Gabriel.

As she rode along, she saw Mr Boldwood with Gabriel Oak and one of her other farm workers. The three of them seemed to be talking about something very important. They stood there for a few more minutes, and then Boldwood and Gabriel walked away, while the third man came towards Bathsheba.

When he reached her, she said, 'Well, Joseph, what's the news?'

'Fanny Robin died in the workhouse. She has to be buried in our churchyard by law, so Mr Boldwood is going to send a cart this afternoon to bring her back here for burial.'

'Oh, I won't let Mr Boldwood do that. Fanny was my uncle's servant. I'll do it,' said Bathsheba. 'How long had she lived at the workhouse?'

'Only a day or two. She'd been in Melchester. She walked all the way from there to Casterbridge on Saturday night.'

'Ah!' Suddenly Bathsheba understood.

When she got home, she said to Liddy, 'What colour was Fanny's hair?'

'It was real golden hair.'

'Her young man was a soldier, wasn't he?'

'Yes. Mr Troy told me that he and Fanny's young man looked so like each other that people sometimes thought they were the same person.'

Joseph cheers up

Joseph drove a cart to Casterbridge workhouse that afternoon. At three o'clock the coffin was put in, and he drove back to Weatherbury.

5   He felt very sad to be driving along with a dead body in his cart. When he reached an inn, he stopped to have a drink to cheer himself up. Inside, he saw two of his friends from the farm, Coggan and Clark. They drank and talked for some time. Then Joseph said that he had to

10 go.

'What's your hurry?' Coggan said. 'The woman's dead. You can't bring her to life again. You might as well sit here in comfort and enjoy another mug with us.'

At six o'clock they were still there, when heavy

15 footsteps were heard outside the inn. The door opened, and Gabriel came in. He looked severely at the three men, who by then were all quite drunk. 'Really, I'm ashamed of you all,' he said.

'Don't be like that, shepherd!' begged Clark.

20 'Nobody can hurt a dead woman,' said Coggan. 'Why hurry for a thing that can neither feel nor see?'

'Stop talking nonsense!' said Oak. 'And you, Joseph, you're as drunk as you can be.'

Gabriel could see that none of the three men could

25 drive a cart now, so he just went out and drove the cart home himself.

The news that Fanny was going to be buried that day had slowly spread through the village, but nobody knew exactly what had happened. Gabriel hoped that the whole

30 truth would not come out until Fanny had been in her grave for a few days. In that way the news would affect Bathsheba less severely.

As Gabriel stopped the cart in front of the farmhouse, the village priest came out.

35 'Have you brought the dead woman?' he asked.

'Yes, sir,' answered Gabriel.

'I just came to ask Mrs Troy why it was so late. We can't bury her tonight. We'll have the funeral tomorrow morning. You can take the body to the church, or leave it here.'

Gabriel did not want to leave the body at Bathsheba's house. All kinds of unfortunate results might follow, he thought. But first he had to ask Bathsheba's permission to take it to the church. He told her that it would be easier to go straight there, and leave the body in the cart.

Bathsheba disagreed. 'It wouldn't be kind or respectful to leave poor Fanny outside in the cart all night,' she said. 'Bring the coffin into the hall.'

Gabriel went to find three men to help him. Between them they carried the coffin inside. Everyone left except Gabriel. He was still worried that something might happen to make Bathsheba discover some fearful truth.

Suddenly, in a last attempt to save Bathsheba from at least immediate pain, he looked at the words that had been written in chalk on the coffin. He saw that they said 'Fanny Robin and child'. He took his handkerchief and carefully rubbed out the last two words. Then he quietly went out of the house.

Wicked stories

Troy had been out since early morning. Bathsheba was sitting downstairs, waiting for him to return, when Liddy came in.

'Do you want me any longer, madam?' she asked.

'No more tonight, Liddy. But just tell me what you know about Fanny. Was she very ill?'

'Not very.'

5   'She's been away from us for about eight months. Did anyone ever say that she wouldn't live long?'

'I never heard anyone say so.'

'Have you heard anyone say she had some kind of illness?'

10   'No, madam. Have you?'

'Oh, no, no. I only asked because I was curious. Surely people who are ill can't walk a very long distance the day before they die.' Then suddenly she was sorry that she had said this, and began to cry.

15   Liddy, who was looking at the weeping woman with astonishment, said 'Why are you crying like that, madam? Has anything I said hurt you?'

'No, Liddy. I don't know why I've begun to cry so much recently. I never used to cry. Good night.'

20   Liddy went out and closed the door.

Bathsheba was lonely and miserable. She was fighting a battle inside herself. For the past few days she had been worrying about her husband's past. She had been angry with Fanny because Fanny was loved by the man whom 25 she herself still loved, even though that love was being weakened by new worries and suspicions. Now, however, Fanny was dead, and Bathsheba thought she should feel sympathy for the poor woman instead of being angry.

Not long afterwards Liddy came in again. She said, 30 'Maryann says she heard something strange about Fanny, but I am sure it can't be true …'

'What is it?'

'Oh, just a wicked story she heard in the village. Some people are saying that there are two of them out there!' 35 Liddy indicated the coffin in the hall by a movement of her head.

Bathsheba's whole body trembled.

'Two of them? I don't believe it!' she said. 'And there's only one name on the coffin.'

'I don't believe it either, madam, but I thought I should tell you. Someone heard Oak say that the story was about another poor girl, and I believe him. We would surely have been told about it if it had been true, don't you think, madam?'

'We might, and then we might not. Please leave me alone, now.'

Bathsheba looked away so that Liddy would not see her face as she left the room.

Bathsheba sees for herself

Bathsheba was now even unhappier than ever. She could guess the truth. Neither Oak nor Boldwood realized how much she knew. A few days before she had seen Troy helping a lonely woman. Oak knew nothing of this. He was doing all he could to save Bathsheba from pain. If he had known of that meeting, he would have allowed the truth to come out immediately.

Suddenly Bathsheba needed to speak to someone who was stronger than herself. She knew that Oak was strong — stronger even than Boldwood, she had discovered to her surprise. She felt sure that Oak knew everything she wanted to know about Fanny.

She put on a cloak and walked slowly to Gabriel's cottage. But when she got there, she lost her courage. After standing outside Gabriel's door for some time, she turned and went back home.

In the hall she stopped to look at Fanny's coffin. She said, 'I wish you could speak and tell me your secret, Fanny! Oh, I hope it isn't true that there are two of you! If only I could look in on you for one little minute, I would know.'

A few moments passed, and then she added slowly, 'And I will!'

She went and got a screwdriver. In a short time the coffin had been opened, and Bathsheba had seen what lay inside. She stood there, trembling.

'It was best to know the worst, and I know it now,' she
5 said to herself.

It had all been done as if in a dream. Now she had absolute proof of her husband's behaviour. In the coffin, beside Fanny, she could see the small face of a baby. And she could see that Fanny's hair was a golden yellow. There
10 was no longer any doubt about whose hair it was that Troy kept in the back of his watch.

Bathsheba cried. Her tears fell fast beside the coffin. Wild thoughts began to race through her mind. Fanny had had Troy's child. She had triumphed over Bathsheba.

15 Bathsheba now thought everyone would despise her. She would escape from her shame by killing herself at once. But even this would just be a poor copy of what Fanny had done.

Troy is confused

20 As she looked at the two dead bodies, she exclaimed excitedly, 'Oh, I hate them … No, I don't mean that I hate them, because it is wicked to do that … But I do hate them a little! Yes, my heart insists on hating them, whether my mind is willing to or not. If only she had lived, I could
25 have been angry with her and cruel to her with some justice, but to feel this way about a poor dead woman and her baby only harms me. Oh, I am so miserable about all this!'

Suddenly her husband appeared at the hall doorway.

30 Troy looked around slowly, and was speechless with surprise. It was as if he had seen a ghost. Bathsheba looked back at him in the same wild way. In his confused state of mind, Troy thought that someone in the house had died. He had been out all day, and had not heard the
35 news. He did not realize it was Fanny in the coffin.

'Well — what?' he said, unable to think clearly.

'I must go — I must go,' said Bathsheba, speaking to herself more than to him. She went towards the door, trying to push past him.

'In God's name, what's the matter? Who's dead?'

'I cannot say — let me out! I need air!'

'No — stay here!' He seized her by the hand, and pulled her back with him to the side of the coffin.

Troy looked into it at the faces of mother and baby. Then he let go of his wife's hand as he suddenly understood everything. He stood there looking into the coffin, very still.

His real wife

Troy remained like that for some minutes. He seemed to have lost all power or wish to move. His various feelings were fighting each other so strongly that his brain seemed to be frozen.

At last Bathsheba spoke. 'Do you know her?'

'Yes.'

'Is it she?'

'It is.'

Now he sank down on his knees, with a look of the greatest sadness on his face. He bent down and gently kissed Fanny Robin, as one would kiss a sleeping child.

This was too much for Bathsheba. She jumped forward. Her anger had changed to a deep sorrow; the union between herself and the man she loved had now been broken. She threw her arms round Troy's neck, exclaiming wildly from the depths of her heart, 'Don't — don't kiss her! Oh, Frank, I can't bear it! I love you better than she did — kiss me, too, Frank — kiss me!'

Troy pulled her arms from his neck and looked at her in surprise. He could hardly believe that his proud wife, Bathsheba, could behave so childishly. After all, her rival was now dead.

He pushed her away, saying, 'I shall not kiss you. This woman is more important to me, even now that she is dead, than you ever were, or are, or can be. If the devil had not tempted me with your pretty face, and your pretty way of saying things, I would have married her. I never thought of anything else till I met you. I wish to God that I had — but it is all too late!' Then he turned to Fanny and said, 'But it doesn't matter, my darling. In the sight of Heaven you are my real wife.'

At these words Bathsheba gave a low cry of despair. It was the end of her union with Troy.

'If she's that, then what am I?' she asked, crying.

'You are nothing to me — nothing,' said Troy coldly. 'A wedding in a church doesn't make a marriage. I was never really yours.'

Bathsheba's only wish now was to run away from him, and from that place. She wanted to hide and to escape his words at whatever cost, even if it meant death. Without waiting a moment longer, she turned and ran out of the house.

10

TROY DISAPPEARS

The attic

Bathsheba hurried along the dark road, neither knowing nor caring where she was going. She reached a wood. She went in among the trees and lay down on some soft, dead leaves. 5

She was not sure whether she slept or not during that night, but when she became fully conscious again, it was morning. She felt anxious, and then hungry and thirsty.

Someone now appeared on the hill opposite the wood, and Bathsheba recognized Liddy. She felt deeply grateful 10 that she had not been completely forgotten.

'Liddy!' she called out.

'Oh, madam,' the girl said, 'I'm so glad that I've found you!' She came towards her mistress, and said, 'Poor thing! Cheer up a little, madam. How ever did —?' 15

'Did anyone send you, Liddy?'

'Nobody. When I realized that you weren't at home, I thought something cruel had happened.'

'Is Mr Troy at home?'

'No, he left shortly before I did.' 20

'We won't go home yet.'

'But madam, you need to eat something. And you'll catch your death of cold sitting out here.'

'I shan't come in yet — perhaps never.'

'Shall I get you some food, and a cloak?' 25

'Please, Liddy.'

Liddy went, and returned twenty minutes later with a cloak, a hat, bread and butter and some hot tea in a jug. She said that the men were just taking Fanny's body to the church. She had told everyone that Bathsheba was ill 30 and could not be disturbed — they all thought she was still in her bedroom.

In about ten minutes the two women returned to the farmhouse, going in by the back door. Bathsheba crept up a small stairway to an empty attic, and Liddy followed.

'Liddy, I'll live up here for a while.'

5   All that day Bathsheba and Liddy stayed in the attic with the door locked, but this proved to be unnecessary, because Troy did not appear.

A cursed life

Troy had left the house that morning. He walked towards
10   the churchyard, and searched there until he found the grave that had been dug for Fanny. Then he hurried off to Casterbridge. He went to a stonemason's yard that made tombstones. There he saw a beautiful tombstone that was nearly finished. All that needed to be done was to have
15   the name carved onto it. Troy paid twenty-seven pounds for it — that was all the money he possessed.

That evening, when it was quite dark, he walked to the churchyard, carrying a basket. By then the stonemason's men had brought the tombstone and put it in place at the
20   head of Fanny's grave. Troy knelt down, took from his basket the roots of flowers of various kinds, and began to plant them on the grave.

When he had nearly finished, a big drop of rain fell on his lamp. The light went out. It began to rain heavily, and
25   he went to the church to take shelter. He sat down on a bench just inside the entrance and fell asleep.

At the top of the tower of Weatherbury Church there were four gargoyles. Their purpose was to allow rain-water to drain off the roof through their mouths. Three of
30   them were broken, and blocked. All the rain water drained out of the one good one.

As Troy slept, the rain fell more and more heavily. Soon the gargoyle began to spit water. The water beat on the bare earth. It ran straight into Fanny's grave. Soon the flowers that Troy
35   had planted were floating around in a roaring pool of water.

Troy did not wake until the
next morning. He took his
basket and went out. He
saw with a shock that all
his work on Fanny's grave
had come to nothing. The
plants had gone, and in
their place was a big hole.

To Troy this was the
sharpest pain of all. He had
tried to calm his conscience by
these gifts to the dead woman he
had loved. Now fate had defeated him. For
the first time in his life, he wished he was another
man. He hated himself, and felt that his life was cursed.   15

Slowly he left the grave, without trying to fill up the
hole or put the flowers back. He walked away from the
church and away from the farmhouse. Soon he had left
Weatherbury village, too.

Bathsheba sees the tombstone   20

Meanwhile Bathsheba stayed in her attic. The door was
always kept locked except when Liddy went in or out. In
the morning Liddy suggested that Bathsheba might like to
go and see Fanny's grave, but her mistress was afraid that
she might meet her husband there.   25

'Has Mr Troy been in tonight?' she asked.

'No, madam. I think he's gone to Budmouth. Joseph
saw him on the Budmouth road early this morning.'

Bathsheba felt relieved, and decided to walk to the
graveyard. When she got there, she saw a grave with a   30
beautiful stone on it, and a big hole below. There were
splashes of mud on the gravestone. On the other side of
it stood Gabriel. His eyes were also fixed on the tomb.
He had not heard Bathsheba coming, because she was
walking very quietly.   35

Bathsheba did not think that such a beautiful stone could be on the grave of a poor person like Fanny, so she looked around for something more ordinary. But then her eyes followed Gabriel's and she read:

5   *Put up by Francis Troy in Loving Memory of Fanny Robin.*

Oak looked to see how she would feel about these words, which had astonished him greatly. But Bathsheba had had so much pain that she could not feel anything any more. She said, 'Good morning,' to Gabriel, and asked him to fill in the hole in the grave.

While he did this, she collected the flowers and began planting them. Then she asked Oak to tell the church officials to turn the gargoyle so that next time the water from it would go somewhere else. Finally she wiped the mud from the tombstone, and went home again.

Carried out to sea

Troy wandered off, but not to Budmouth, as people had said. He felt that it would be too painful for him to remain in Bathsheba's house, or even in Weatherbury.

He came to Lulwind Cove, a small town by the sea which was a favourite place for visitors in the summer. Troy felt happier now. He decided to bathe before going on. He took his clothes off and jumped into the water. It was very calm, so he swam out to enjoy his swimming more. Unfortunately he was caught there by a current which took him to the left, and then in a curve far out to sea.

When he realized what was happening, he remembered that many swimmers had been drowned at Lulwind Cove. He began to believe that he might join them. He tried for a long time to get back to land, but the current was very powerful. When he was almost too tired to swim any more, a ship's boat suddenly appeared in the distance.

Troy shouted and waved to it, and the sailors saw him at once. In a few minutes they had reached him, and pulled him into their boat.

Each of the men took off a piece of his own clothing and gave it to Troy. Troy told them his story. He asked them to take him back to where he had left his clothes.

Because of the current, it took a long time to get there, and when they arrived, it was dark. Troy anxiously looked for his clothes, but they had gone. 15

'All I possess has gone,' he said to the sailors. 'I haven't a friend in the world, and I have no money!'

'If you get into the boat again,' they said, 'we can find you some clothes. We need more sailors, and our captain might give you work.' 20

Troy thought for a moment. The sailors would hardly let him go away with the clothes they had lent him, and he could not pay for them.

'How long will I have to work?' he asked.

'The older sailors have signed on for two years. The 25 captain would probably want you to work for at least six months, perhaps longer.'

Troy accepted. It would be best for everyone if he left the country, he thought.

The boat began to move off, and after some time Troy 30 could see lights on the sea, and then the dim shapes of ships. One of them would be his new home.

Doubts

Bathsheba was surprised, and then relieved as her husband's absence increased from hours to days. She was 35 only the tenant of her farm. When her uncle had died, the owners of the place had been doubtful about letting a woman keep the farm, but the way in which Gabriel had organized the sheep had won their confidence.

5 But Bathsheba's marriage to Troy had raised new doubts. If she lost the farm, she would lose everything. She realized that her marriage had been a mistake. She accepted that, and waited, calmly, for what would result.

The first Saturday after Troy's departure, Bathsheba

10 went to Casterbridge alone. While she was walking in the town, someone came up to her and said,

'I have some unpleasant news for you, Mrs Troy. I am afraid your husband has drowned.'

As if she had the power to see the future, Bathsheba

15 cried out, 'No, it isn't true; it can't be true!' Then a darkness came over her eyes, and she fell. But not to the ground. Someone who had been watching her stepped forward quickly to her side and caught her in his arms as she sank.

'What is it?' said Boldwood, holding Bathsheba and

20 looking up at the man who had brought the news.

'Her husband was drowned earlier this week while swimming in Lulwind Cove. Someone found his clothes and brought them to Budmouth yesterday.'

A strange fire suddenly came into Boldwood's eyes. His

25 face grew red with excitement. He lifted Bathsheba up and carried her to the nearest inn, where he put her on a sofa. She opened her eyes at the same moment and whispered, 'I want to go home.'

Boldwood offered to take her in his carriage, but she

30 refused politely, and he left. About half an hour later she felt strong enough to drive back home herself.

The news had already reached Weatherbury. Bathsheba said nothing to anyone when she returned. She went up to her bedroom and remained there for the rest of that

35 day. Later Liddy knocked at the door and came in. 'You will need to get some black clothes,' she said.

'What for?'

'Mourning.'

'No, no, no,' Bathsheba objected.

'Why not, madam?'

'Because Mr Troy is still alive. I'm sure of it.'

She was not quite so sure on the next Monday, when
Troy's clothes arrived. Also there was a report in the
newspaper from a young doctor who had seen a man in
difficulties in the sea near Lulwind Cove.

Then Bathsheba began to think that perhaps Troy had
decided to follow Fanny into another world, and had
drowned himself intentionally. She opened Troy's watch.
The piece of golden hair was still in it. She took it out
and held it over the fire.

'No — I won't burn it — I'll keep it in memory of that
poor girl!' she said, pulling her hand back quickly.

Oak becomes bailiff

Autumn and winter came, and Bathsheba continued to
lead a quiet but not really peaceful life. While she knew
that Troy was alive, she had been able to think of his
death calmly. Now that it seemed that she might have lost
him, she regretted it.

One very good result of her general lack of interest in
life was the appointment of Oak as farm bailiff. He had
in fact been doing the work of a bailiff for a long time
already, so this did not make much difference to him,
except that he got better wages.

Boldwood seldom went out, and he neglected his farm
completely. However, when Bathsheba made Oak her
bailiff, Boldwood suddenly decided to ask Oak to look
after his farm, too. At first Bathsheba objected to this, but
as the two farms were side by side, and Boldwood was
willing to provide Oak with a horse, everything was finally
settled in a friendly way.

Bathsheba paid Oak a fixed wage. Boldwood arranged
to give him a small share of his profits, too. Some people

began to think that Oak was mean, because, although he was now getting a lot more money, he continued to live a very simple life.

A great hope had now grown in Boldwood's mind. He was still madly in love with Bathsheba. His hope was that she might now be willing to marry him.

Summer and autumn came again. One day Boldwood met Liddy, and after exchanging greetings, he asked her how Bathsheba was. When Liddy told him, he said, 'Mrs Troy trusts you very much, Liddy.'

'Yes, sir. And even if she married again, I expect I would stay with her.'

These words filled Boldwood with hope that his darling was thinking about remarrying.

'She's told you that, I suppose,' he said.

'No — she hasn't promised it exactly, but that's what I think.'

'Yes, I understand that. I mean, when she talks about marrying again —'

'Oh, she never mentions it, sir. I was just trying to say how much she trusted me.' Liddy was beginning to think that Mr Boldwood was becoming rather stupid.

His hopes fell. He added, 'Well, it's very wise of her to decide never to give up the freedom she now has.'

'My mistress did once say that she might marry again at the end of seven years from last year. Until then she would have to risk Mr Troy coming back and claiming her.'

'Any reasonable person would agree that she could marry now, if she wanted to, whatever the lawyers may say against it.'

'Have you asked them?' Liddy asked.

'Oh, no!' Boldwood blushed, and then he quickly said, 'Goodbye,' and left Liddy.

Boldwood was angry with himself and ashamed at having asked Liddy such dishonest questions. But he also now had the hope that in six years' time, Bathsheba might marry him.

TROY RETURNS

At the sheep fair

About two years later, Bathsheba and Boldwood went to the fair at Greenhill. The fair was held once every year, and was a great occasion. Farmers and dealers came from all around to buy and sell animals and products of all kinds. More business was done there in a few days than in all the rest of the year put together. Also there were many other attractions. In a large tent in the centre of the fair, some actors from a travelling circus were performing a play. It was about Dick Turpin — a famous thief. In the play Turpin had to ride a horse, and people said the actor who took the part of Turpin was a very clever rider. He could shoot accurately, too, and was a good swordsman. Everyone wanted to see him.

Boldwood had been hoping to speak to Bathsheba privately all day. In the middle of the afternoon he at last saw his chance, and walked across to her.

'Did you get a good price for your sheep, Mrs Troy?' he asked hesitantly.

'Oh, yes, thank you,' she answered. She looked very uncomfortable speaking to Boldwood. 'I was lucky enough to sell them all soon after we arrived.'

'And now you have nothing more to do.'

'I have to see one more dealer in two hours' time, or else I would be going home now. Have you ever seen the play about Turpin that they are doing here?'

'Oh, yes. I saw it last year. You haven't, I suppose.'

'Never. I wasn't allowed to go to such things when I was young.'

'Would you like to see it now? I can get you a seat.'

Bathsheba hesitated, so he went on quickly, 'I myself shall not stay to see it — I've seen it before.'

Bathsheba did want to see the play, but she had been afraid to go in alone. She had been hoping that Oak would appear, but she could not see him anywhere. So she said, 'If you will look in first to see if there's room, then I think I will go in for a minute or two.'

And so a short time after this, Bathsheba appeared in the tent with Boldwood. He took her to a special bench for the richer people. She was the only person on that bench. The ordinary people had paid half the amount of money that her seat had cost Boldwood, and they had to stand, but they could see much more. Even worse, all these people now turned to look at her.

Recognized!

Before the play started, the actor who was playing Turpin looked through a small hole in the side of his tent and was shocked to see Bathsheba. The actor was Troy. He had finished working as a sailor. He had lived in America for a short while, and had now returned to England.

Troy knew that Bathsheba would not recognize his face, because he would be wearing a big, black beard, but he was sure she would recognize his voice. Also she looked so beautiful that he began to think about going back to her, which surprised him. But he then realized that, if she saw him now, she would despise him more than ever because of the low job he was doing.

He hurried to the manager of the circus and said, 'There's a man in the tent to whom I owe money. As soon as I start talking, he'll recognize my voice. He'll get the police to arrest me and have me put me in prison.'

The manager did not want to lose his best actor. He said, 'All right. Turpin doesn't have to say much. We'll pretend that you don't have to say anything at all.'

The play went well, even though Turpin said nothing. Then that evening there was a second performance. This time Troy noticed that one man in the audience was watching him very closely. It was Bathsheba's first bailiff, Pennyways — the man she had dismissed for stealing.

Troy thought this man had probably recognized him. After the play had ended, he decided that it would be wise to make a friend of Pennyways if possible.

The note

The best place to eat at the fair was a big refreshment tent. Troy, still wearing his thick, black beard, went there and looked in. He saw Bathsheba there, so he went out again and walked round to the back of the tent, just behind the place where she was sitting. There he made a small cut in the tent so he could watch her.

Bathsheba was talking to Boldwood, who had brought her a cup of tea. Again Troy was surprised to feel a sudden rush of love in his heart for his wife. She was as beautiful as ever, and she was his. For a moment he thought he might go and claim her, but he did not want anyone to know that he was working in a circus. If he returned to Weatherbury to live, he would have to keep that a secret.

Bathsheba was just taking out her purse and insisting on paying Boldwood for her tea when suddenly Troy saw Pennyways enter the tent. Troy trembled. He had wanted to meet the man first. Now he was too late. Pennyways went to Bathsheba and said, 'Excuse me, madam, but I've got some private information for you.'

'I don't have time to talk to you now,' she answered the man coldly. It was clear that she disliked him. In fact he often came to her with stories about other people, to try to win back her favour.

'I'll write it down,' Pennyways said. He tore a piece of paper out of an old notebook and wrote down the words, 'Your husband is here.' He held the note out to Bathsheba, but she refused to take it. With a scornful laugh, he then
5 threw the note onto the table in front of her, and left.

A good joke

Troy had not been able to read what the man had written, but he had heard his words. He could not think of any way of stopping Bathsheba finding out the truth. 'Curse
10 my luck!' he whispered.

Boldwood picked up the piece of paper. 'If you don't want to read it, Mrs Troy, I'll destroy it,' he said.

'Oh, well,' Bathsheba said carelessly, 'perhaps I ought to read it. But I don't suppose it is anything important.'
15 She took the note in her right hand, but before she could open it, Boldwood offered her a plate of bread and butter. Bathsheba put out her left hand to take it, and, for a moment, dropped her right hand to her side.

At once Troy lifted up the bottom of the tent, pulled the note from her hand and quickly ran away.

Bathsheba screamed in astonishment.

A minute or two later, Troy came back quietly to the refreshment tent as if nothing had happened. He wanted to find Pennyways to stop him talking about what he had seen.

In the tent several people were talking about a bold attempt that had just been made to rob a young lady. They thought it was a good joke. The thief, they said, had only stolen a piece of paper instead of the banknote he had probably expected, or the lady's purse.

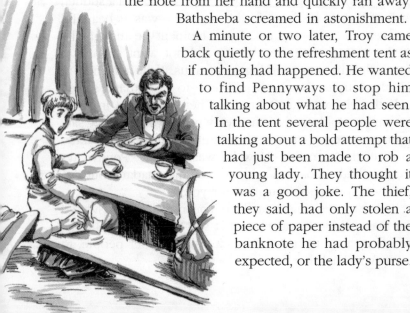

After looking around for some time, Troy found
Pennyways. He went up to him, whispered a few words,
and the two men left the tent together.

The promise

When Bathsheba was ready to drive home in her carriage,   5
Boldwood offered to ride along beside her on his horse.
She was frightened after what had just happened, so she
was glad of his company. This gave him new hope.

They went along in silence for a while. Then, he said,
'Mrs Troy, will you marry again some day?'   10

This direct question confused her. A minute or more
passed before she answered, 'I haven't thought about it.'

'I understand. But your husband has been dead for
nearly a year now, and —'

'His death was never absolutely proved. I may not really   15
be a widow.'

'That's true, but a man saw him drowning. No one really
doubts that he is dead — not even you, madam, I think.'

'Oh, yes, I do. If not, I would have behaved differently.
From the beginning I've had a strange feeling that he   20
could not have drowned. Even if I were half sure that I'd
never see him again, I'd not think about marrying anyone
else. People would scorn me for thinking such a thing.'

'I shall never stop regretting the things that prevented
me from marrying you.'   25

'And I am sorry you thought that I might marry you.'

'If I had real proof that you were a widow, would you
correct the wrong that you did me, and marry me now?'

'I don't know.'

'But you might?'   30

'I might.'

'Well, do you know that in six years' time the law allows
you to marry again without needing any more proof?'

'Oh, yes, I know that,' she answered quickly. 'But who
can say where we shall all be in six years' time?'   35

'But if I wait, will you marry me then?'

'Please let us not talk about it any more.'

'Of course, if you wish; but promise that, if you decide to marry again, it will be me!'

He was so excited that she was almost afraid of him.

'I will never marry another man while you wish me to be your wife,' she said.

'Promise me that you will be my wife in six years' time.'

'Oh, what can I do?' she said sadly. 'I don't love you; but if you know that, and can still be happy with my promise to marry you in six years' time, then, at Christmas, I will give you that promise.'

Christmas Eve

For the next few weeks, Bathsheba was in a strange state of mind. She felt that she had been forced into saying she would give Boldwood her word. As Christmas came nearer, her anxiety increased.

One day, when she was working on the farm accounts with Gabriel, the subject came up again. Speaking of Boldwood, Gabriel said, 'He'll never forget you, madam.'

Then, before she really knew why, she was telling Gabriel the whole story. 'The real reason for saying what I did,' she said, 'was that I was afraid that if I did not give him my word, he would go insane. I believe I hold that poor man's future in my hands. It frightens me so!'

Christmas Eve arrived. Everybody in Weatherbury was talking about the party that Boldwood was giving that evening, and to which he had invited many people. Christmas parties at Boldwood's house were most unusual.

As Bathsheba was dressing for the party, she said to Liddy, 'I wish I didn't have to go to this party, but I can't escape it now. I am the reason why he is giving the party, and that worries me.'

At about the same time, Oak arrived at Boldwood's house to report on the day's work. Oak said, 'I'm glad to see you looking so much happier, Mr Boldwood.'

'Yes,' said Boldwood, 'I'm feeling very cheerful. Perhaps my luck is changing at last. And as the world is becoming brighter for me, I want to increase your share of the farm's profits. I know a secret about you, Gabriel. Your interest in Mrs Troy is more than that of a bailiff for his employer. But you have behaved perfectly, and I, as a kind of successful rival — successful partly because of your help — would like to show my feeling of friendship to you in what must have given you great pain.'

'Oh, that isn't necessary,' said Oak hurriedly. 'I must get used to unhappiness, as other men do.'

Oak then left. Boldwood went to his desk and unlocked a drawer. He took out a small box and opened it. It contained a woman's ring with diamonds on it. It looked as if it had been bought quite recently.

Troy at this time was having a drink in an inn near Weatherbury, and talking to Pennyways.

'Did you see the lawyer?' Troy asked.

'No, he wasn't in.'

'I don't think that because a man seemed to be drowned but wasn't, he owes anybody anything.'

'Ah, but that isn't the important thing. If a man changes his name and tries to deceive his wife and everyone else, he's dishonest and can be punished.'

'Well, what I really want to know,' Troy said anxiously, 'is what is happening between her and Boldwood. Have you found out anything?'

'No, I haven't.'

Troy got up and began putting on a big coat, with a collar that came up nearly to his cap.

'Nobody will recognize me in this, I'm sure,' he said.

'You've really decided to go back to her?'

'Yes, of course.'

'If I were you, I'd do nothing: a good wife is good, but the best wife is not so good as no wife at all.'

'Nonsense!' said Troy. 'She has plenty of money and comfort, and I'm living in poverty.' And he left the inn.

A CHANGED WOMAN

Boldwood's happiness

Later that evening, a carriage arrived at Boldwood's house. Boldwood himself hurried to open the door, and the light shone on Bathsheba.

5 Boldwood was highly excited. Bathsheba had come to his party, and later, in front of everyone there, she would make her promise to marry him. It would be a great occasion. However, he did his best to control his feelings. He just welcomed Bathsheba warmly, like a good host.

10 Bathsheba could not make up her mind what to do. Sometimes she thought that she shouldn't have come at all; then she realized that that would have been too unkind. Finally she decided to stay for only an hour and then leave quietly.

15 When the hour had passed, she went into a small room to get ready to leave. There was nobody else in the room, but she had hardly been there a moment when Boldwood entered.

'Mrs Troy,' he said, 'you aren't going so soon? We've
20 hardly begun.'

'If you'll excuse me, I'd like to go now.'

'I've been trying to get an opportunity to speak to you,' said Boldwood. 'Perhaps you know what I'm eager to say.'

Bathsheba looked at the floor silently.

25 'You do give it?' he said eagerly.

'What?' she whispered.

'Now you're avoiding answering! Your promise, of course. A promise to marry me at the end of five and three-quarter years. You owe it to me!'

30 'I feel that I do, if you demand it. But I am a changed woman — an unhappy woman.'

'You're still a very beautiful woman.'

'I give my promise if I must, but only, of course, if I'm a widow. I give it as the payment of a debt.'

'You'll marry me between five and six years from now?'

'Don't press me too hard. I promise that I'll marry nobody else.'

'Say the word, dear one, and I'll say no more about it for six years,' he pleaded.

She was so upset that she began to weep. 'All right,' she said when she could speak again. 'If he doesn't return, I'll marry you in six years from today if we're both alive.'

'And you'll take this to remind you?'

He came close to her, took her hand and showed her the ring.

'Oh, no, I can't wear a ring!' she exclaimed. 'I don't want anyone to know. Don't insist, Mr Boldwood.'

'It is just a promise — no feelings,' he said more quietly, still holding her hand tightly. He put the ring on her finger.

'I can't wear it!' she said, weeping bitterly. 'You frighten me, Mr Boldwood. Please let me go home!'

'Wear it only tonight to please me.'

At last she said in a hopeless whisper, 'All right then, I will wear it tonight, if you wish it so much. Now please take your hand off mine.'

Boldwood pressed her hand and then allowed it to drop in her lap. 'I'm happy now,' he said. 'God bless you!'

'Go with your husband!'

When Bathsheba felt calm enough to leave, she came downstairs. To get to the front door, she had to pass through the hall where the party was. As she was doing so, there was a loud knocking.

A servant went to the front door. Soon he came back and following him was Troy, wearing his big coat and cap. Bathsheba saw him. She leant against the wall, her face very pale, her mouth open and her eyes fixed on him.

Boldwood did not recognize Troy at first. He said, cheerfully, 'Come in, come in!' and offered him a drink.

Troy came forward. He took off his cap and turned the collar of his coat down, but it was not until he began to
5 laugh that Boldwood recognized him.

Troy turned to Bathsheba. Her unhappiness was now absolute. She had sunk down onto a chair, her mouth blue and dry, her dark eyes fixed on him as if she thought he was some terrible ghost.

10 'Bathsheba, I've come here for you,' said Troy.

She did not answer.

'Come on. Come home with me.'

She did not move.

'Come, madam, do you hear what I say?'

15 A strange voice was heard — a voice that sounded as if it came from inside a cave a long way off. It was Boldwood's.

'Bathsheba, go with your husband!' he said.

Still she did not move. Her brain seemed to be frozen.

20 Troy put out his hand to pull her towards him, and now she moved back. Her fear of him seemed to annoy Troy. He seized her arm and pulled her sharply forward. She twisted her body and gave a quick, low scream.

A moment later there was a sudden deafening bang, and the hall filled with grey smoke.

When Bathsheba had screamed, Boldwood's despair had changed. An insane look had come into his eyes. He had turned quickly, taken one of the guns from the wall behind him, and shot Troy.

Troy fell. A sigh came from him, his body twisted, and then he lay still.

Boldwood could now be seen getting ready to shoot himself, too, but one of his men ran forward and pulled the gun away. In the struggle the gun went off, but it fired harmlessly into the ceiling.

'Well, it makes no difference,' Boldwood gasped. 'There's another way for me to die.'

Then he crossed the room to Bathsheba, kissed her hand, and went out into the darkness. Nobody tried to stop him. He went straight to Casterbridge Prison and gave himself up as the murderer of Francis Troy.

The heart of a wife

Oak had not been present at the party, but he was one of the first to hear the terrible story, and he hurried to Boldwood's house. He found everyone in a state of great shock. No one knew what to do.

Bathsheba was in despair. She was sitting on the floor beside the body of Troy, and had placed his head on her lap. She had put her handkerchief over his wound, and was holding one of his hands tightly in one of hers. She seemed no longer frozen with panic, and she was surprising everyone by her calmness and control.

'Gabriel,' she said, 'ride to Casterbridge at once to get a doctor. I think it's useless, but go.'

The doctor did not reach Boldwood's house until three hours later. By then Troy had died, and Bathsheba had taken his body to her own house.

The doctor drove there, and was met at the door by Liddy. 'Where is your mistress?' he asked.

'Upstairs, sir. She locked herself in her room with him.'

Oak arrived just then with the priest and they all went upstairs together. Liddy knocked at her mistress's door, and Bathsheba opened it. They all went in, and saw a body at the other end of the bedroom, wrapped in white.

The doctor went to examine it, and when he returned, he said, 'The body has been cleaned and made ready for burial. This girl must have the spirit of the bravest soldier.'

'Just the heart of a wife,' came a whisper. The men
5 turned and saw Bathsheba as she silently sank down to the floor in a faint.

They took her into another room. The doctor, who had been unable to help Troy, was of the greatest value to Bathsheba. For some time she was in a dangerous
10 condition.

After the men had gone, Liddy heard Bathsheba whisper again and again, 'Oh, it is my fault, it is all my fault — how can I live?'

Thinking of leaving

15 Three months later the time came for Boldwood to be tried for the murder of Troy. Shortly before the trial, a strange discovery was made. People already suspected that Boldwood might be mad. Now, in a locked cupboard in his house, an extraordinary collection of articles was
20 found. There were several expensive dresses, and some fine jewellery. They were carefully wrapped in paper. On each package was a card which said, 'Bathsheba Boldwood', with a date that was six years in the future.

Boldwood pleaded guilty to murder, and received
25 sentence of death. However, people were sure that he had not been responsible for his behaviour because he was mad. They asked the Government to review the sentence, in the hope that he would not be hanged. After some weeks of anxiety, the news came that Boldwood would
30 not receive the full punishment of a murderer, but would be sent to a prison-hospital for the insane.

Bathsheba was very ill. Slowly she began to get well again, but she remained alone most of the time.

Summer came, and one evening in August she decided
35 to go for a walk. She went to the church, and visited the

grave where both Fanny and Troy were now buried. As she read Troy's name on the tombstone, she began to cry, and once she had started, she could not stop.

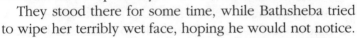

She did not notice a man coming quietly to the entrance of the church. On seeing her, he stopped and watched her. When at last she raised her head, her face wet and her eyes drowned in tears, she said in surprise, 'Oh, Mr Oak! How long have you been there?'

'Just a few minutes, madam,' he answered respectfully.

They stood there for some time, while Bathsheba tried to wipe her terribly wet face, hoping he would not notice.

'Were you coming to the church?' he asked at last.

'No, I was coming to see whether they had put the words that I had asked for on the tombstone. And now I'm going home, Mr Oak.' 20

'May I speak to you about some farm business?' he asked.

'Yes.' 25

'It's about me. I'm thinking of leaving England and going to America.'

'But I've heard that you've been offered Mr Boldwood's farm.'

'Yes, but I have reasons for going.' 30

'But Gabriel, what will I do without you? We've been through good times and bad times for so long, and we're such old friends. Now that I'm more helpless than ever, you want to go away.'

'Yes,' answered Gabriel in a worried voice, 'it's because 35 of your helplessness that I feel I have to go. Goodbye, madam.' He hurried away.

At Oak's house

During the following weeks, it was clear to Bathsheba that Oak was avoiding her. At last the thing that she had been fearing most came — a formal letter from Oak giving
5 notice that he could no longer work as her bailiff.

She cried bitterly over the letter. She was deeply hurt that Oak's hopeless love for her, which she considered to be her right for life, was going to be taken away. She felt so full of despair that she went to Oak's house.

10 'You'll think it strange that I've come,' she said, but —'

'Oh, no, not at all.'

'But I thought you were leaving because I had offended you, and that made me very sad.'

'Offended me? You couldn't do that, Bathsheba.'

15 'Couldn't I?' she answered. 'Then why are you leaving?'

'I'm not going to leave England. I've arranged to have Mr Boldwood's old farm for myself, so I shall still be close by. I wouldn't have wanted to stop working for you either, if people hadn't started talking about us.'

20 'What are they saying?' Bathsheba asked in surprise.

'I can't tell you.'

'It would be wiser if you did.'

'They say that I'm waiting here because I think I may get you some day.'

25 'Get me? What does that mean?'

'Marry you. You asked me to tell you, so you mustn't blame me.'

Bathsheba did not look as shocked as Gabriel had expected. 'Marrying me? Such a thing is too silly — I mean
30 too soon — to think of.'

'Yes, of course it's too silly, as you say.'

'I said too soon, not too silly.' There were tears in her eyes now.

Gabriel came closer and looked deep into her eyes.
35 'Bathsheba,' he said tenderly, 'I wish I knew that you would allow me to love you and marry you after all!'

'But you never will know!'

'Why?'

'Because you never ask! You should never have sent me that cruel letter this morning, because you were the first man who loved me, and I can never forget it!'   *5*

'Now, Bathsheba, I wrote you that letter because I thought that people might talk if I, as a man who was not married, was doing business with a very attractive woman like you. Nobody knows how that worried me.'

'And was that all?'   *10*

'Yes.'

'Oh, how glad I am that I came,' she exclaimed. 'But I must go now.'

As they went to the door, she said with a laugh, 'You know, it seems exactly as if I had come here trying to get   *15* you to marry me — how terrible!'

'And quite right, too,' said Oak. 'I've followed you and helped you for a long time, my beautiful Bathsheba, so you really owed me this visit.'

The secret wedding   *20*

'We shall have the most private, secret, simplest wedding that anyone can have.' Those had been Bathsheba's words to Oak one evening some time after this.

The morning of the wedding, Liddy, who had been told nothing, was surprised to find her mistress dressed when   *25* she went to wake her up at seven o'clock.

'What's happening, madam?' she asked.

'Well, I'll tell you,' answered Bathsheba with a naughty smile. 'Farmer Oak is coming to dinner with me tonight.'

'You two alone? Is that safe after what people are   *30* saying?'

Bathsheba laughed and whispered in Liddy's ear. Liddy's eyes opened wide, and then she said, 'Heavens, what news! It makes my heart jump and jump!'

'Mine too,' answered Bathsheba.   *35*

At ten minutes to ten that morning, Oak arrived at Bathsheba's door, and they walked together to the church. The only other people there were the priest, the church clerk and Liddy, and in a few minutes the whole thing was finished.

In the evening of the same day, Bathsheba and Oak were having tea in her house when they heard the sound of a cannon firing, and after that a band began to play in front of the house.

Oak went to the door with Bathsheba. They saw a group of men standing outside, and behind them many people from the village. When they saw the newly married couple at they door, they all cheered, and at the same time the cannon, which had been in the village for many years, fired again. There then followed a frightful burst of music from the village band.

When they had finished, Gabriel asked them in for something to eat and drink. They thanked him, but refused, saying they would call at a more suitable time. They wished Oak and his beautiful wife long life and much happiness.

'Thank you, thank you all,' said Gabriel. 'I thought we might get a visit from our old friends, and was saying so to my wife just now.'

Someone said Gabriel had learned to say the words 'my wife' in a surprisingly natural way for a man who had been married such a short time. Then Oak laughed, and Bathsheba smiled (for she never laughed easily now), and their friends turned to go.

QUESTIONS AND ACTIVITIES

CHAPTER 1

Which of these sentences are true? In the false sentences, what is wrong with the underlined parts?

1 Gabriel thought that <u>the woman in the cart was vain</u>.
2 He thought this <u>because she argued about money</u>.
3 Gabriel employed <u>some rich landowners on his farm</u>.
4 Mrs Hurst was frightened <u>because her cow was so ill</u>.
5 Bathsheba was offended <u>because Gabriel had seen her behaviour on the horse</u>.
6 Gabriel nearly died <u>from staying outside in the cold</u>.
7 Gabriel went to Mrs Hurst's <u>to thank Bathsheba for saving his life</u>.
8 Bathsheba ran after Gabriel <u>to say she wanted to marry him</u>.
9 She was almost angry with Gabriel for agreeing with her idea <u>that he ought to marry a rich woman</u>.

CHAPTER 2

Put these sentences in the right order. The first one is done for you.

1 Oak went to Casterbridge fair to look for work.
2 Bathsheba gave him a job as a shepherd.
3 He did not find any work there.
4 He saw some ricks burning.
5 He helped put the fire out.
6 He went on to Weatherbury.
7 At the inn the men asked him to play his flute.
8 On his way he met a girl with an attractive voice.
9 The bailiff said he might find lodgings at the inn.

CHAPTER 3

Who said these things, and to whom were they speaking?

1 'You now have a mistress instead of a master.'
2 '... don't you know me? I'm your wife ...'
3 'Did you notice Mr Boldwood in church ..?'
4 '... this will be a nice surprise for him.'
5 'The men have been talking about the strange things the new mistress is doing.'
6 '... the first man that I hear saying bad things about our mistress will smell and taste this!'
7 'If you haven't read this letter, you'd better do so.'

CHAPTER 4

Use these words to fill in the gaps: **Bathsheba, Boldwood, Everdene, French, Lord, Oak, Robin, Sergeant, Troy**.

Sergeant (1) _____ 's mother was (2) _____, and she had an affair with (3) _____ Severn. Fanny (4) _____ wanted (5) _____ Troy to marry her. Mr (6) _____ had helped her as a child, so he was interested in her. He had received a valentine from Miss (7) _____, but it did not have a name on it, so he asked Gabriel (8) _____ whose writing it was. Then he wanted to marry (9) _____, but she did not want to marry him.

CHAPTER 5

Choose the best answers.

1 When Bathsheba and Gabriel were together, she did all the talking, which meant nothing because: (a) she did not love Gabriel; (b) she felt nervous; (c) she was stupid.
2 Gabriel, on the other hand, was silent, which meant a lot because: (a) he did not like Bathsheba; (b) he did not want to interrupt Bathsheba, because this would be rude; (c) he loved Bathsheba but did not want to show it.
3 Bathsheba kept her eyes fixed on the ground when Boldwood was talking to her about: (a) Gabriel; (b) his wish to marry her; (c) the shearing.

4 Bathsheba criticized Gabriel for wounding a sheep while shearing because: (a) she was angry that he was so careless; (b) she thought it was the sheep's fault; (c) she guessed Gabriel had been watching her and Boldwood.

CHAPTER 6

*Use these words to fill in the gaps: **bees, crest, curses, hair, insect, kiss, kisses, ladder, swarm, sword, watch**.*

Sergeant Troy said he preferred (1) _____ from Bathsheba to (2) _____ from any other woman. He gave her a gold (3) _____ with a family (4) _____ on it. One day he helped Bathsheba to catch a (5) _____ of (6) _____ by climbing up a (7) _____. Then he showed her some exercises with a (8) _____, and cut off a piece of her (9) _____ with it, and then killed an (10) _____ with it. Before he left her, he gave her a (11) _____ on her mouth.

CHAPTER 7

Put the letters of these words in the right order to describe Bathsheba's drive to Bath.

Gabriel and Coggan thought someone had (1) **elonts** a horse. They rode towards a (2) **lolt-teag**. Coggan said he was sure they would (3) **thacc** the thief. He knew that the keeper there was the (4) **stepilees** man between Bath and (5) **onnoLd**. They found they had been following Bathsheba. She said that (6) **attinprom** business had made it (7) **sascenery** for her to go to Bath at once. She had given up her (8) **sitiv** to Liddy and taken a horse and a (9) **greriaca**.

CHAPTER 8

Find and correct the ten mistakes in this description of how Oak saved the ricks.

Oak saw that the ricks were not finished. He knew that if they got very cold, the corn would be useful. He went back to the farmyard to get help, but all the people there were busy, so he returned and put four large covers over four ricks. He took a crook and used it to arrange some sheep on top of the other ricks to protect them. While he was doing this, the storm suddenly began, and a flash of thunder showed that Liddy had arrived to help him.

CHAPTER 9

Put the beginning of each of these sentences with the right ending.

1	Joseph went to Casterbridge	(a) to drive the cart home.
2	He stopped at an inn	(b) to see if there was a baby in it.
3	Oak left the inn	(c) to get Fanny's coffin.
4	Bathsheba was waiting	(d) to have a drink and cheer up.
5	She opened the coffin	(e) for Troy to return.

CHAPTER 10

Put the underlined (b) sentences in the right paragraphs.

1 (a) That evening Troy walked to the churchyard carrying a basket. (b) <u>There were splashes of mud on it.</u> (c) Troy knelt down and began to plant flowers on the grave.

2 (a) When Troy woke the next morning he had a shock. (b) <u>By then the stonemason's men had placed the tombstone at the head of Fanny's grave.</u> (c) The plants had gone, and in their place was a big hole.

3 (a) When Bathsheba got to the churchyard, she saw a beautiful gravestone. (b) <u>All the work he had done on Fanny's grave had come to nothing.</u> (c) On the other side of the gravestone stood Gabriel.

CHAPTER 11

Choose the right words to describe what this part of the story is about.

Greenhill fair was a great (1) **situation/occasion**. More business was done there in a few (2) **days/months** than in the rest of the (3) **country/year** put together. In the centre of the fair was a large (4) **barn/tent**, where some (5) **actors/robbers** were taking part in a (6) **carriage/play** about Dick Turpin. One of them could shoot (7) **accidentally/accurately**, and he was also a good (8) **manager/swordsman**. This man was Troy, who had now returned from (9) **America/Australia**.

CHAPTER 12

Put the names of these people in the right places. The name of a place will appear in the centre column. Choose from: **Farmer, Liddy, Robin, Boldwood, Gabriel, Bathsheba, Everdene, Troy, Hurst, Sergeant, Oak**.

Bathsheba's first husband was (2)_____ (4)_____.
(5)_____ (10)_____ married the right man in the end.
(6)_____ (3)_____ waited a long time to marry the woman he loved.
(7)_____ (1)_____ killed Bathsheba's first husband.
Fanny's surname was (8)_____.
Bathsheba's aunt was Mrs (9)_____.
(11)_____ was Bathsheba's favourite servant.

Oxford
Progressive
English Readers